Living The Jedi Way

Michele Doucette, M. Ed.

Living The Jedi Way

ISBN 978-1-935786-27-6

Printed in the United States of America by

St. Clair Publications

PO Box 726

McMinnville, TN   37111-0726

http://stclairpublications.com/

Table of Contents

Dedication

Jack Layton, Leader of the Official Opposition as well as the Leader of the New Democratic Party (NDP), was the most honest, authentic, devoted politician that Canada has seen within the last four decades. Clearly, he was a visionary well ahead of his time.

As you delve into the heart of this book, I think many will agree that he was truly a Jedi Master.

If I may share his parting words ... *My friends, love is better than anger. Hope is better than fear. Optimism is better than despair. So let us be loving, hopeful and optimistic and we'll change the world.*

I hope that many will take the time to read Jack Layton's final letter to the Canadian people. [1]

---

[1]

http://beta.images.theglobeandmail.com/archive/01310/Jack_Layton_s_lett_1310744a.pdf

Introduction to the Star Wars saga

There are a great many individuals that resonate with this American epic series created by George Lucas.

Star Wars Episode I: The Phantom Menace

Released on May 19, 1999, *The Phantom Menace* was the fourth film to be released in the Star Wars saga, both as the first of a three part prequel to the original Star Wars trilogy, as well as the first film in the saga in terms of story chronology. The film follows Jedi Master Qui-Gon Jinn and his apprentice Obi-Wan Kenobi, who escort and protect Queen Amidala in traveling from the planet Naboo to the planet Coruscant in the hope of finding a peaceful end to a large scale interplanetary trade dispute. Along the way, they meet Anakin Skywalker, a young slave boy who seems to be unusually strong with nascent powers of the Force, and must contend with the mysterious return of the Sith. [2]

Star Wars Episode II: Attack of the Clones

Released on May 16, 2002, *Attack of the Clones* was the fifth film to be released in the Star Wars saga and the second in terms of internal chronology. The longest film in the series, it runs for 142 minutes. The film is set 10 years after the events in *The Phantom Menace*, when the galaxy is on the brink of civil war. Under the leadership of a renegade Jedi named Count Dooku, thousands of planetary systems threaten to secede from the Galactic Republic. When an assassination attempt is made on Senator Padmé Amidala, the former Queen of Naboo, 20-year-old Jedi apprentice, Anakin Skywalker, is assigned to protect her, while his mentor Obi-Wan Kenobi is assigned to investigate the assassination attempt. Soon, Anakin, Padmé, and Obi-Wan

---

[2]

http://en.wikipedia.org/wiki/Star_Wars_Episode_I:_The_Phantom_Me
nace

are drawn into the heart of the Separatist territories and the beginning of a new threat to the galaxy, the Clone Wars. [3]

Star Wars Episode III: Revenge of the Sith

Released on May 19, 2005, *Revenge of the Sith* was the sixth and final film to be released in the Star Wars saga and the third in terms of internal chronology. The film takes place three years after the onset of the Clone Wars. The Jedi Knights are spread out across the galaxy leading a massive clone army in the war against the Separatists. The Jedi Council dispatches Jedi Master Obi-Wan Kenobi to eliminate the evil General Grievous, leader of the Separatist Army. Meanwhile, Jedi Knight Anakin Skywalker, separated from Kenobi, his former master, grows close to Palpatine, the Chancellor of the Galactic Republic and, unbeknownst to the public, a Sith Lord. Their deepening friendship proves dangerous for the Jedi Order, the galaxy,

---

[3]

http://en.wikipedia.org/wiki/Star_Wars_Episode_II:_Attack_of_the_Cl ones and Anakin himself, who inevitably succumbs to the Dark Side of the Force and transforms into Darth Vader. [4]

Star Wars Episode IV: A New Hope

At the time of its initial release on May 25, 1977, I was in Grade 10.

The first to be released (as *Star Wars*) and the fourth in terms of internal chronology, this film follows a group of freedom fighters, known as the Rebel Alliance, as they plot to destroy the powerful Death Star space station, a devastating weapon created by the evil Galactic Empire. This conflict disrupts the isolated life of farm boy Luke Skywalker when he inadvertently acquires the droids carrying the stolen plans to the Death Star. After the Empire begins a cruel and destructive search for the droids, Skywalker decides to accompany Jedi Master Obi-Wan Kenobi on a daring mission to rescue the owner of the

---

[4]

http://en.wikipedia.org/wiki/Star_Wars_Episode_III:_Revenge_of_the_Sith

droids, rebel leader Princess Leia Organa, and save the galaxy. [5]

Star Wars Episode V: The Empire Strikes Back

At the time of its release on May 21, 1980, I was in my last month of High School.

The second to be released (as *The Empire Strikes Back*) and the fifth in terms of internal chronology, the Galactic Empire, under the leadership of the villainous Darth Vader, is in pursuit of Luke Skywalker and the rest of the Rebel Alliance. While Vader chases a small band of Luke's friends (Han Solo, Princess Leia Organa, and others) across the galaxy, Luke studies the Force under Jedi Master Yoda. When Vader captures Luke's friends, he must decide whether to complete his training, and become a full Jedi Knight, or confront Vader in order to save his comrades. [6]

---

[5] http://en.wikipedia.org/wiki/Star_Wars_Episode_IV:_A_New_Hope

[6] http://en.wikipedia.org/wiki/Star_Wars_Episode_V:_The_Empire_Stri kes_Back

Star Wars Episode VI: Return of the Jedi

At the time of its release on May 25, 1983, I was halfway through my University training as a Special Education teacher.

The third to be released (as *Return of the Jedi*) and the final in terms of internal chronology, it was the first film to use THX technology. The evil Galactic Empire, with the help of the villainous Darth Vader, is building a second Death Star in order to crush the Rebel Alliance. Since Emperor Palpatine plans to personally oversee the final stages of its construction, the Rebel Fleet launches a full-scale attack on the Death Star in order to prevent its completion and kill Palpatine, effectively bringing an end to the Empire. Meanwhile, Luke Skywalker, a Rebel leader and Jedi Knight, struggles to bring his father, Darth Vader, himself a fallen Jedi, back from the Dark Side of the Force. [7]

---

[7]

http://en.wikipedia.org/wiki/Star_Wars_Episode_VI:_Return_of_the_Jedi

Matthew Bortolin, author of <u>The Dharma of Star Wars</u>, uses this series to illustrate Buddhist concepts (such as suffering, mindfulness, karma and transcending the dark side) that serve to highlight deeper themes within the Star Wars series. In keeping, Jedi meditation can be compared to the Buddhist practice of mindfulness meditation; something that I endeavor my best to practice every day.

According to Yoda, a renowned Jedi Master, a Jedi's strength *flows from the Force.* He also cautions Luke Skywalker against anger, fear and aggression because *fear is the path to the dark side,* meaning that *fear leads to anger, anger leads to hate, and hate leads to suffering.*

When Luke wonders how he will come to know the good side from the bad, Yoda tells him that *a Jedi uses the Force for knowledge and defense, but never for attack.*

Remaining calm and at peace, while engaging in both rational thought as well as meditation, is touted, herein, as the path to enlightenment (as opposed to the dark side of violent passion and erratic emotion).

The strongest influence within this series is Taoist philosophy, second to Zen Buddhism (which, it is said, inherited much from Taoism).

John Porter, author of <u>The Tao of Star Wars</u>, uses motifs from the Star Wars series to explain the basic tenets of Taoism. He integrates his own personal practice of Taoism with the practice of Aikido (a Japanese martial art that allows one to blend with the motion of the attacker, thereby redirecting the force of the attack, rather than opposing it, head-on).

It is within this volume that the light and dark side of the Force are analogous to the Yin and Yang duality of the Tao; likewise, the Force is also comparable to both Tai Chi and Qi Gong.

In accordance with Taoist annals, practitioners of Taoism and Qi Gong can live upwards of 200 years.

Taoism emphasizes smooth flow of the Qi, originating from a balance of the Yin and Yang forces, in all manifestations of life, including both human anatomy and the environment.

Jon Snodgras, author of <u>Peace Knights of the Soul</u>, offers a book that is an in-depth analysis of the spirituality and metaphysics of the two Star Wars trilogies. George Lucas was greatly influenced by the writings of mythologist Joseph Campbell; hence, Jonathan Young, Campbell's long-time assistant and archivist, provides an introduction in the book.

Jediism is a religious movement based on the philosophical and spiritual ideas depicted in the Star Wars series.

While I do not adhere to any religious movement, Jediism, or the Jedi Realist movement, is followed by thousands of people world-wide. It is also recognized as an official religion in Canada, a movement that is a combination of Eastern philosophy meshed with metaphysics, psychology, and Judeo-Christian teachings.

I am, however, intrigued by the comparisons that can be drawn between some of their tenets of belief and my own personal writings.

The Force

As per findings that were published in the October *Astrophysical Journal*, researchers discovered proof of a vast filament of material that connects our Milky Way galaxy to nearby clusters of galaxies, which are also similarly interconnected to the rest of the Universe. [8] This team included Dr. Stefan Keller, Dr. Dougal Mackey and Professor Gary Da Costa from the Research School of Astronomy and Astrophysics at the Australian National University (ANU).

"By examining the positions of ancient groupings of stars, called globular clusters, we found that the clusters form a narrow plane around the Milky Way, rather than being scattered across the sky," Dr. Keller said. "What we have discovered is evidence for the cosmic thread that connects us to the vast expanse of the Universe." [9]

---

[8] http://www.physorg.com/news/2011-09-cosmic-thread-revealed.html
[9] Ibid.

While the Force is described as being the binding, metaphysical and ubiquitous, power in the fictional universe of the Star Wars galaxy saga, created by George Lucas, I see the Force as being synonymous with the Unified Field (with other names being Consciousness, Consciousness Grid, Source of Creation, Oneness, Unity, Nature's Mind, Mind of God and Quantum Hologram, to cite but a few).

The unified field, according to modern physics, is "the deepest, most powerful level of Nature's functioning, and the source of the infinite creativity and intelligence within every individual, displayed throughout the universe." [10]

Gregg Braden, in The Divine Matrix, talks about the universe having been founded on four characteristics; namely, [1] that there is a field of energy that connects all of creation (discovery 1); [2] that this field takes on the role of a container, a bridge and a mirror for the beliefs as held by the individual (discovery 2); [3] that this field is nonlocal and holographic, meaning that every part of it is connected

---

[10] The Unified Field: The Key to Enlightenment, National Invincibility and World Peace website accessed on March 16, 2011 at http://www.america.unifiedfieldconferences.org/

to another, with each piece mirroring the whole on a smaller scale (discovery 3); and [4] that we communicate with this field through the language of emotion (discovery 4). [11]

Gregg Braden is not the first to suggest that coherent emotion is the language that this field of energy understands; Esther and Jerry Hicks, through the words of Abraham, also feel the same way.

"Coherent emotion happens when what we are thinking, feeling, and expressing, are all in alignment." [12] Of course, this means that incoherent emotion can be described as "the kind of emotion we experience when we are feeling one way, thinking another way, and expressing something different, from either our thoughts or our feelings." [13]

---

[11] Braden, Gregg. (2007). *The Divine Matrix: Bridging Time, Space, Miracles and Belief* (page xxi). Carlsbad, CA: Hay House, Inc.
[12] *Oneness and The Unified Field* article accessed on March 16. 2011 at http://www.escapetheillusion.com/blog/2008/10/oneness-and-the-unified-field-gregg-braden/
[13] Ibid.

When you think about something, further coupled with feelings and emotions, you are sending out powerful vibrations.

Everything is connected, meaning that your vibrations affect everyone, directly or indirectly.

Everything you do (what you are thinking, what you are feeling, what you say, how you behave) is vibrated into the universal field (universal consciousness) of which you are a significant particle of source energy.

Knowing that each is affected by the other is what further demonstrates the interconnectivity (transpersonal consciousness) that exists between all of us.

In keeping with the unified field, it must be remembered that each of us is also part of God.

This means that we are "not simply a part of the Earth; we *are* the Earth. We are not simply a part of the Force that governs all Creation; we *are* that Force." [14]

Consciousness, then, can be said to originate from the very fabric of this unified field.

In returning to the words of Gregg Braden, at the opening of this particular chapter, as individuals, we are constantly creating effects on every part of creation because it is consciousness that permeates every aspect of the unified field. We operate very much like radio transmitters and receivers, sending out signals (vibrations), courtesy of the electromagnetic field that surrounds us.

Since collective consciousness "is created by the individuals within it, as individual consciousness grows, collective consciousness rises; and as collective consciousness rises, individual consciousness grows. In other words, as an individual regularly experiences self-referral consciousness

---

[14] Bolsta, Phil. (2009). *Gregg Braden on Prayer and the Unified Field* posting accessed on March 16, 2011 at http://bolstablog.wordpress.com/2009/12/06/braden-video/

and enlivens it in his own awareness, the levels of collective consciousness in which he participates (family, city, province, nation, etc.) are simultaneously improved. This higher value of collective consciousness, in turn, effects, in a positive way, every one of the individual members of that level of collective consciousness." [15]

The unified field of consciousness is "the essence and source of creation of everyone, regardless of race, age, gender, background, richness or poverty, place and time. Whatever we individually think, experience or believe, we are all conscious beings sharing the same essence." [16]

However, it becomes the beliefs that we have about ourselves, the beliefs to which we have become ingrained and attached, that create the sense of separation that is felt.

Clearly, *we are the source of our own perceived limitations.*

---

[15] Maharishi Vedic University (1999) website. *The Maharishi Effect* article accessed on March 17, 2011 at
http://www.vedicknowledge.com/Maharishi_effect.html
[16] The Unified Field – The Consciousness of All Creation website accessed on March 17, 2011 at
http://www.anunda.com/paradigm/unified-field.htm

Anything that one does to enhance their lives in the here and now, can only serve to also benefit the unified field to which all are connected.

The Force also refers to Life Force Energy.

In Japan, they call it *ki*.

The Chinese, referring to it as *chi,* have actually been able to map its movement throughout the physical body (courtesy of the meridians).

Yoga adepts from India cite its name as *prana*.

In the West, Dr. Wilhelm Reich, upon discovering the same energy, labeled it o*rgone energy*.

Russian researchers, in turn, have termed it *bio-plasmic energy*.

The knowledge that our bodies are filled with life force energy (referenced by any of the names denoted above) and that this life force energy is directly connected with our health ...... such has been part of a wisdom that has been in existence for thousands of years.

The amount of life force energy within your body varies from day to day, depending on a multitude of factors: the foods you eat, the liquids you drink, the air you breathe and the energy you absorb through your auric field, to cite just a few, noteworthy, elements.

This life force energy can be found everywhere. Given that it is the connective force of the universe, so, too, is there a limitless supply.

There are three main sources of life force energy, as paraphrased below. [17]

[1] Solar: required for approximately 20 minutes each day (either before 11:00 AM or after 3:00 PM), this invigorating form promotes good health (vitamin D).

[2] Air: absorbed into the lungs through breathing, this life force energy is absorbed by the energy centers of the body (chakras). Deep, slow, rhythmic breathing allows one to absorb more life force energy than short, shallow breaths.

---

[17] http://www.healing-journeys-energy.com/Chi.html

[3] Ground: absorbed through the soles of the feet, meaning, of course, that walking barefoot increases the amount of life force energy absorbed by the body. Availing of more ground energy, in connecting with Mother Earth, increases your vitality levels, allowing you to think more clearly.

When your life force energy is high, you feel healthy, fit, strong and full of stamina; you also feel confident, ready to take on the challenges that present themselves to you.

By comparison, when your life force energy is low (given the fact that there is either a restriction or a blockage in its flow), you feel weak, tired, listless and lethargic.

This is when one is more vulnerable to illness and/or disease; especially if the energy depletion continues to last for a considerable period of time. It is important, therefore, to learn how to replenish your life force energy.

To understand healing from a Buddhist perspective, the mind is the creator of sickness and health.

If mind (meaning both thought as well as consciousness) is the creator, as many of us believe, then *the cause of disease is internal* as opposed to external.

Buddhism asserts that "everything that happens to us now is the result of our previous actions, not only in this lifetime, but in other lifetimes. What we do now determines what will happen to us in the future," [18] meaning that in order to heal present (as well as future) sickness, we have to engage in positive actions now.

Buddhism also states that "for lasting healing to occur, it is necessary to heal not only the current disease with medicines and other forms of treatment, but also the cause of the disease, which originates from the mind. If we do not heal or purify the mind, the sickness and problems will recur again and again." [19]

---

[18] *Healing: A Tibetan Buddhist Perspective* article accessed on March 23, 2011 at http://www.buddhanet.net/tib_heal.htm
[19] Ibid.

It becomes in "ridding the mind of all its accumulated garbage, all of the previously committed negative actions and thoughts, and their imprints, [that] we can be free of problems and sickness permanently. We can achieve ultimate healing: a state of permanent health and happiness. In order to heal the mind, and, hence the body, we have to eliminate negative thoughts and their imprints, and replace them with positive thoughts and imprints." [20]

Many have stated the basic root of our problems, which may also include sickness, to be selfishness (the inner enemy) in that selfishness "causes us to engage in negative actions, which place negative imprints in the mindstream. These negative actions can be of body, speech or mind, such as thoughts of jealousy, anger and greed. Selfish thoughts also increase pride, which results in feelings of jealousy towards those higher than us, superiority towards those lower than us, and competitiveness towards equals. These feelings, in turn, result in an unhappy mind, a mind that is without peace. On the other hand, thoughts and actions directed to

---

[20] *Healing: A Tibetan Buddhist Perspective* article accessed on March 23, 2011 at http://www.buddhanet.net/tib_heal.htm

the well-being of others bring happiness and peace to the mind." [21]

Another powerful method, in Buddhism, is "to meditate on the teachings known as thought transformation. These methods allow a person to see the problem or sickness as something positive rather than negative. *A problem is only a problem if we label it a problem.* If we look at a problem differently, we can see it as an opportunity to grow or to practice, and regard it as something positive. If someone gets angry at us, we can choose to be angry in return or to be thankful to them for giving us the chance to practice patience and purify this particular karma. It takes a lot of practice to master these methods, but it can be done." [22]

The compassionate mind is a calm, peaceful, joyful and stress-free environment; a mental environment that is ideal for healing.

---

[21] *Healing: A Tibetan Buddhist Perspective* article accessed on March 23, 2011 at http://www.buddhanet.net/tib_heal.htm
[22] Ibid.

It was Norman Vincent Peale, a pastor at the Marble Collegiate Church in New York City, who wrote an extremely popular book, The Power of Positive Thinking, a book that urged "ordinarily Americans to employ mind-body ideas to help themselves." [23]

It was Norman Cousins who wrote The Anatomy of an Illness (as Perceived by the Patient) in which he "told how he defeated his own severe physical ailment through laughter (including watching Marx Brothers movies)." [24]

Eastern medicine practices, like Chinese medicine and Ayurveda, have long embraced the concept of mind and body being interlinked, while we, here in the west, still prefer to treat both body and mind as separate units.

However, "several scientists and researchers are beginning to acknowledge the mind's role in healing and looking to

---

[23] *The Cure Within: Can the Mind heal the Body?* article accessed on March 22, 2011 at http://www.mindpowernews.com/CureWithin.htm
[24] Ibid.

leverage the effects of a positive state of mind in order to create better health." [25]

If a thought has been thought repeatedly for a long time, it becomes a belief. Dr. Bruce Lipton, an internationally recognized cellular biologist and author of the book, The Biology of Belief, believes that, "genes are actually manipulated by a person's belief system. It means that genes don't themselves cause a condition, except when they are triggered by the environment composed of one's thoughts, emotions and beliefs." [26]

Dr. Christiane Northrup, author of Women's Bodies, Women's Wisdom, denotes that "emotions and thoughts are always accompanied by biochemical reactions" [27] in the body, meaning that the "cells in our bodies are memory banks that have imprints of events that the conscious mind might be unaware of. To create health, one must decide to

---

[25] *Do Diseases Originate in the Mind? Can Emotions Heal the Body?* article accessed on March 22, 2011 at http://www.suite101.com/content/do-diseases-originate-in-the-mind-can-emotions-heal-the-body-a323062
[26] Ibid.
[27] Ibid.

be happy and make a conscious effort to uncover the programming of the body." [28]

Both examples are insightfully demonstrated scientific connections linking emotions, thoughts and mind to the state of one's health and well-being.

The medical field is finally beginning to acknowledge that the attitude of the patient has a very large impact on how fast that patient heals; so, too, does this include whether he/she survives a certain procedure.

A large number of medical studies are continuing to demonstrate that "negative emotions play a significant role in the development of heart diseases, chronic pain, autoimmune diseases and cancer. Anxiety, anger, shame and sadness drain our energy and suppress our immune system. Stress-related illnesses are the number one cause of death in the US. Self-sabotaging or addictive behaviors

---

[28] *Do Diseases Originate in the Mind? Can Emotions Heal the Body?* article accessed on March 22, 2011 at http://www.suite101.com/content/do-diseases-originate-in-the-mind-can-emotions-heal-the-body-a323062

keep us stuck in old, destructive patterns. Non-supportive self-talk such as *I can't do this* or *I don't deserve this* revent us from accessing our full potential and achieving our goals. On the other hand, positive thinking, a self-empowered attitude and optimistic beliefs, both stimulate and enhance the healing process." [29]

David R. Hamilton acquired an honors degree in biological and medicinal chemistry, and a Ph.D. in organic chemistry, before working as a scientist in the pharmaceutical industry for several years.

His research into the mind-body connection ultimately led him to leave that profession and become a motivational speaker.

The author of How Your Mind Can Heal Your Body, Dr. Hamilton talks about the close and powerful connection between the mind and body.

---

[29] *Accelerated Healing, Change and Self-Empowerment Through Mind-Body-Spirit Integration* article accessed on March 22, 2011 at http://www.cellularwisdom.com/body-mind-healing.shtml

The power of thought can affect you in profound ways, particularly in regards to its truly incredible effect on your health, as is explored in detail within the pages of How Your Mind Can Heal Your Body.

Exploring the power of visualization, belief, and positive thinking, and their effects on the body, Dr. Hamilton presents a revolutionary quantum-field healing meditation (through which you can change yourself on an atomic level), showing you how you can use your imagination and thought processes to combat disease, pain, and illness.

As a result, it is possible for science and belief systems to merge in an effective manner for healing.

Such is the very nature of the Force.

Jedi Training

Matthew Vossler, author of <u>Jedi Manual Basic: Introduction to Jedi Knighthood</u>, shares that training to be a Jedi Knight includes training and practice in ......

[1] meditation, [2] martial arts, [3] the healing arts, [4] psychic awareness and social graces, [5] mediation, diplomacy, and peacemaking, [6] the Jedi philosophy and religion, [7] teaching, coaching, and mentoring, [8] practical skills for defending and protecting others, [9] gentle and objective deliberation, persuasion, and debate, [10] literary and theatrical arts, [11] working with energy and the supernatural, and [12] sustained pursuit of knowledge and wisdom, so as to attain a good measure thereof.

Each of these twelve routes, according to Matthew Vossler, leads to the final path; the goal of a Jedi Knight.

A Jedi can choose to focus on one, or more, of these skills at any given time.

A Jedi becomes a master when they achieve mastery in one, or more, of the 12 paths.

The ultimate goal is to use one, or more, of these masteries to better serve others.

Let us now take the time to look at each separate discipline in more detail.

Meditation

Meditation is an inwardly oriented, personal practice, whereby individuals focus on training both attention and awareness in order to bring one's mental processes under greater voluntary control, [30] which is what serves to foster general mental well-being and development and/or specific capacities such as calm, clarity, and concentration. [31]

---

[30] http://en.wikipedia.org/wiki/Meditation
[31] Ibid.

Meditation has been linked to changes in metabolism, blood pressure and brain activation. Likewise, it has also been used in clinical settings as a method of stress and pain reduction.

Jon Kabat-Zinn is the founder of the Mindfulness-Based Stress Reduction program (MBSR), [32] [33] a program that allows an individual to learn how to use their innate resources and abilities to respond more effectively to stress, pain and illness.

It has been scientifically documented that meditation enhances overall psychological health while also preserving a positive attitude towards stress.

There are different forms of meditation.

Meditation may be done while sitting, but there are also moving forms of meditation (such as Tai Chi, Qigong, Aikido and walking).

---

[32] http://www.umassmed.edu/cfm/about/index.aspx
[33] http://www.umassmed.edu/Content.aspx?id=41254&LinkIdentifier=id

Transcendental Meditation involves repeating a word or phrase, called a mantra, either silently or aloud.

Mindfulness meditation involves one's observation of sensations, perceptions and thoughts (as they arise), but without judgment.

Visualization allows one to focus their thoughts on a specific place or situation.

Guided Imagery is based on the premise that the body and mind are connected; hence, this can be referred to as a program of directed thoughts and suggestions that guide your imagination toward a relaxed, focused state that may aid healing, learning, creativity and performance.

Meditations that focus on words or images, and do not strive for a state of thoughtless awareness, are sometimes called quasi-meditative. [34]

34

http://www.intelihealth.com/IH/ihtIH/WSI/8513/34968/362173.html?d=dmtContent

Free Meditations [35]

Frequently Asked Questions about Meditation [36]

How to Meditate [37]

Learning Meditation [38]

Master Meditation [39]

Meditation Center [40]

Meditation for Health [41]

Meditation and Mental Culture [42]

Meditation Retreats [43]

---

[35] http://www.freemeditations.com/
[36] http://dharma.ncf.ca/faqs/meditationFAQ.html
[37] http://www.how-to-meditate.org/
[38] http://www.learningmeditation.com/
[39] http://www.mastermeditation.com/
[40] http://www.meditationcenter.com/
[41] http://www.meditationforhealth.com/
[42] http://dharma.ncf.ca/introduction/meditation.html
[43] http://www.retreatsonline.com/guide/meditation.htm

Meditation Techniques [44]

Primordial Sound Meditation [45]

Stress Management [46]

The Meditation Den [47]

The Meditation Site [48]

What Is Meditation [49]

Martial Arts

Martial arts, a term that refers to various sports or skills, mainly of Japanese origin, began as forms of self-defense or attack, such as Judo, Karate and Kendo.

---

[44] http://www.metaphysics-for-life.com/meditation-techniques.html
[45] http://www.chopra.com/meditation
[46] http://www.mayoclinic.com/health/meditation/HQ01070
[47] http://www.meditationden.com/
[48]
http://www.feedback.nildram.co.uk/richardebbs/meditation/meditation index.htm
[49] http://www.artofliving.org/what-is-meditation

There are many martial arts styles; namely, Japanese and Okinawan Karate styles, other Japanese and Okinawan styles, Korean styles, Chinese styles, Kenpo styles and Kickboxing styles, to highlight a few, [50] [51] [52] [53] [54] all of which are practiced for a variety of reasons, including self-defense, competition, physical health and fitness, as well as mental and spiritual development.

Healing Arts

Too often we live our lives with limiting beliefs, making it even more paramount that we come to realize, accept and acknowledge that we are limitless beings.

How best can we rid ourselves of programmed beliefs?

How best can we rid ourselves of limiting beliefs?

[50] http://startingmartialarts.com/a_list_of_all_martial_arts/a-list-of-all-martial-arts-styles/
[51] http://www.buzzle.com/articles/martial-arts-styles-and-descriptions.html
[52] http://www.martial-arts-info.com/
[53] http://www.usgyms.net/martial%20arts%20types.htm
[54] http://martialartsites.com/styles.cfm

Some choose to work with affirmations (which only work as long as you *believe* and *feel* what you are saying). It is much too easy to sabotage affirmations if what you are saying and feeling is not in alignment with each other.

Some may attempt guided meditation. Others create vision boards. Speaking for myself, I was relieved to discover Mind Movies, [55] an absolutely phenomenal metaphysical *multi-media tool* that allows you to create a vision of what you want, scored with your favorite song; the one that makes you feel good, the one that makes you want to dance, the one that makes you smile and sing along.

If we are not successful in neutralizing these limiting beliefs, we are not in a position to open up to allowing the universe to bring forth that which we really want.

It is important to remember that *all we experience has been, and continues to be, attracted by us*, depending on our thoughts, feelings, emotions and intent.

_____

[55] http://www.mindmovies.com/?10107

According to quantum physics, the physical world is created by its observer (namely, us). This energy, then, becomes structured into the matter that we see in the physical world, depending on our own individual expectations. The world around us is reflected in what we believe.

It is absolutely imperative that you completely eliminate several powerful words from your vocabulary – NO, NOT, DON'T, CAN'T, SHOULDN'T, COULDN'T – because the *use of these words merely serves to attract more of what you do not want* into your life.

Our thoughts create our feelings.

Our feelings create our vibrations.

In every moment of every day, we are sending out vibrations. They can be easily identified as negative or positive, by the feeling(s) being experienced.

One can learn to reset their vibrations from negative to positive, just by choosing different words and different thoughts.

Emotional Freedom Techniques (EFT) is a very powerful tool that can be used to *neutralize* fears and blockages. EFT requires tapping certain energy points (meridians) of the body while focusing on an issue that needs to be resolved.

Emotional wellness is key.

Emotional wellness is easily identified when you are able to feel a sense of overall comfort and acceptance with the full range of emotions and feelings that one can experience.

As we strive to meet our emotional needs in a constructive way, we are better able to maintain good mental health, a positive attitude and a strong sense of self.

EFT [56] provides a bridge between two well known healing modalities: meridian based therapies and mind body therapies, blending both disciplines into one procedure.

The cause of all negative emotions is a disruption in the energy system of the body.

---

[56] World Center for EFT (Emotional Freedom Techniques) located at http://www.eftuniverse.com/

Over 5,000 years ago, it was the Chinese who discovered a subtle energy in the body; one that could not be seen, felt or identified with the senses.

Energy disturbances can be located in the physical body *before* actually manifesting into abnormal patterns, thereby disrupting healthy cellular organization and growth.

These meridians are the pathways, or energy highways, if you will, through which both positive and negative energy circulates throughout the body. Connected with every organ in the body, the diminishing of one's *chi*, or life force, leads to poor organ functioning, discomfort and ill health.

Balancing this energy is crucial to living a healthy and peaceful life. EFT tapping serves to help balance, as well as restore, energy blockages connected to the meridian system.

Ho'oponopono is the ancient Hawaiian self-help method that clears the body of toxic energies, thereby allowing for the presence of divine thoughts, words, deeds and actions. It means to *make right*.

According to those who avail of this method, errors are created from thoughts that are associated with painful memories from the past.

In essence, Ho'oponopono offers a way, through love, gratitude and forgiveness, to clear the energy of painful thoughts (errors) which cause imbalance and disease.

Dr. Ihaleakala Hew Len healed an entire hospital of mentally ill people using this technique.

According to Dr. Len, we can either live from memory or from inspiration. Memories are merely old programs that keep replaying themselves, over and over and over again.

When we are fully present in our zero state (the state in which we have zero limits: no memories, no thoughts, no identity), only the divine exists.

All problems begin as thoughts. When you employ Ho'oponopono, the divinity residing within neutralizes and/or purifies these painful thoughts. These thoughts can be related to people, places, events and situations.

In using Ho'oponopono, there are four phrases that you repeat, out loud, to yourself.

I love you (meaning that you are allowing yourself to be open to all of the love that is coming to you).

I am sorry (meaning that you are apologizing to the divinity within for your erroneous program (thoughts) even without knowing the cause).

Please forgive me (meaning that you are asking the divinity within for forgiveness).

Thank you (meaning that you are expressing gratitude for the opportunity that clearing an erroneous program gives to you).

As you repeat these four phrases, you must focus your intent on addressing the divinity within.

As we heal ourselves, we participate in the healing of the world around us. Zero Limits by Joe Vitale is a wonderful book about Ho'oponopono.

There are also additional energetic methods that can be used to clear the meridians of energy blockages.

Reiki is a Japanese technique for stress reduction and relaxation that also promotes healing. Administered by the laying on of hands, it is based on the idea that an unseen life force energy (understood by the Chinese over 5,000 years ago) flows through us.

The practitioner uses his or her hands in the energy field of the client to facilitate healing. The client remains fully clothed and in a laying position. The practitioner usually moves his or her hands at a distance of a few inches from the body, although touching can be involved.

If one's life force energy, or *chi*, is low, we are more likely to get sick or feel stress. If one's life force energy, or *chi*, is high, we are more capable of being happy and healthy.

To learn more, visit The International Center for Reiki Training. [57]

_____

[57] http://www.reiki.org/

<u>Crystal Therapy</u> involves the use of crystals to attempt healing by affecting personal, and environmental, vibration as a means to facilitating balance and healing.

Gems, stones and crystals are generally laid on the body over the chakra points. As each chakra resonates to a particular color, laying a stone of that color over the chakra allows the chakras to open, align and blend with each other, thereby facilitating balance. When the chakra system is balanced, the physical body is able to experience healing.

It has been said that Crystal Therapy is an ancient art, originating, as some believe, in ancient Egypt. Others believe the form to be even older, possibly dating back to both Lemuria and Atlantis.

While I resonate with a great many different stone types, some of my favorite stones are those containing Lithium, such as Golden C, Lepidolite, Kunzite, Hiddenite and Lithium Quartz, in that they serve to assist me in the calming of my anxieties when I am unable to meditate.

In keeping with the lore and metaphysical properties attributed to gems, stones and crystals, while unsubstantiated from a scientific perspective, each individual must assume responsibility for their use of, and/or misuse of, this information.

All matter is comprised of energy. Zero Point energy is formless. Zero Point energy is also the source of everything. Tachyon Energy was the first to emerge out of the energetic continuum. Tachyon energy cannot be measured. It is not limited to a certain frequency.

Everything that transpires within the human body is already encoded within Tachyon energy (or *chi*) in perfect form, meaning that Tachyon represents a safe and most natural possibility for enabling the human body to move back to energetic health and balance.

I am currently exploring Zero Point energy via the Zero Point Continuum of Life Nano Wand. [58]

---

[58] http://zeropointbreakthrough.com/reps/mdoucette/

The result of more than 27 years of research, and based on a synergy of ancient healing wisdom and modern scientific breakthroughs, these powerful Nano Wands are comprised of a proprietary scientific combination of granulated minerals, fused together inside a magnetic casing (high grade stainless steel) to access Zero Point energy.

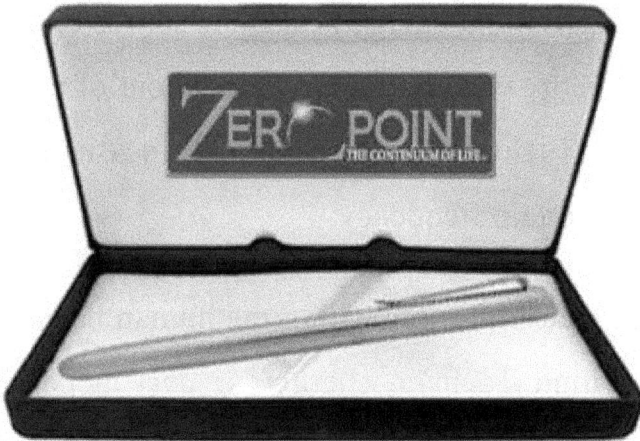

The Nano Wand contains zeolite, tourmaline, germanium, magnetite, hematite, rose quartz, amethyst and a proprietary blend of more than forty other crystals, minerals and elemental ingredients, all of which support the process of scalar energy healing.

The Nano Wand is a natural energy generating device that rejuvenates molecular structures found in all liquids.

With the human body ranging anywhere from 55% to 78% water, depending on physical size, water is the medium that enables the signal of the beneficial energy patterns from the Nano Wand to improve the quality of the body's liquids.

The Nano Wand facilitates and strengthens the flow of bio-energy (also called *chi* or *ki*). It also unblocks areas in which that energy may not be flowing fully. This can have the effect of allowing your body to improve its natural immune response, thereby increasing energy. In addition, the nutrients and micronutrients in the foods you consume can be more effectively utilized.

The Nano Wand is fully endorsed by the Centre for Quantum Healing & Noetic Sciences in Lancaster, Pennsylvania, USA.

Chios Energy Healing, although relatively new, is a very comprehensive energy healing system that employs powerful and effective aura and chakra healing techniques, nearly all of which are unique to Chios.

To learn more, visit the <u>Chios Energy Healing</u> [59] website of founder Stephen H. Barrett.

<u>Therapeutic Touch</u> is an effective healing modality widely used and accepted in clinical practice. It is a modern application of several ancient healing practices which use the laying on of hands.

The practitioner uses his or her hands in the energy field of the client to facilitate healing. The client remains fully clothed and in a laying position. The practitioner usually moves his or her hands at a distance of a few inches from the body, although touching can be involved.

Therapeutic Touch is based on the concept that humans are complex energy fields.

It is the goal of Therapeutic Touch to rebalance the flow of energy as a support to the healing process.

<u>Healing Touch</u> is a bio-field therapy that is an energy based approach to health and healing.

---

[59] http://www.chioshealing.com/

This approach uses touch to influence the human energy system, specifically the energy field that surrounds the body, as well as the energy centers (chakras) that control the energy flow from the energy field to the physical body.

The goal in Healing Touch is to restore harmony and balance to the human energy system. It is most helpful in promoting relaxation, reducing pain and managing stress.

Quantum Touch is a method of natural healing that works with the life force energy of the body to promote optimal wellness.

Life force energy, also known as *chi* (Chinese) or *prana* (Sanskrit), is the flow of energy that sustains all life. Quantum Touch teaches one how to focus, amplify and direct this energy.

All healing is self-healing. The body has an extraordinary intelligence and ability to heal itself. Given the right energetic, emotional, nutritional and spiritual environments, the natural state of the body is that of perfect health.

Although all healing is, indeed, self-healing, Quantum Touch, by combining various breathing and body awareness exercises, can help other people heal with their own healing process.

To learn more, visit the <u>Quantum Touch</u> [60] website.

It was in November of 1957 that "a world famous physician and scientist died in a U.S. federal penitentiary where he had been imprisoned for resisting an unlawful injunction designed to stop his vital research, steal his discoveries, and kill the discovery." [61] This was later proven to be "the culmination of more than 10 years of harassment and persecution at the hands of carefully concealed conspirators who used U.S. Federal Agencies and Courts to defraud the people of this earth and prevent them from knowing and utilizing crucial discoveries in physics, medicine, and

---

[60] http://www.quantumtouch.com/
[61] Bernard, Raymond (1969). *The Hollow Earth* (p 8). Secaucus, NJ: Citadel Press for University Books Inc.

sociology, which could help bring about the happiness and peace for all mankind." [62]

The man in question was Wilhelm Reich; the device being the orgone energy accumulator.

Orgone energy is "the fundamental creative life force long known to people in touch with nature, speculated about by natural scientists as the universal ether, employed by acupuncturists, and finally objectified and scientifically demonstrated by the work of the late Wilhelm Reich, M.D." [63]

It was through years of observation and experimentation that Reich was able to identify "many of the basic properties of the orgone energy: it fills all space and is everywhere; it is mass free; it is the primordial, cosmic energy; it penetrates matter; it pulsates and is both observable and measurable; it has a strong affinity and attraction to/by water; it is

---

[62] Bernard, Raymond (1969). *The Hollow Earth* (p 8). Secaucus, NJ: Citadel Press for University Books Inc.

[63] http://orgonetachyondevices.loveomni.com/orgone%20information.html

accumulated, naturally, in the organism by food, water, breathing and through the skin." [64]

Reich discovered a way to collect or accumulate orgone energy from the atmosphere, using a combination of organic materials (which serve to absorb and hold the energy) meshed with inorganic materials (which serve to attract and then rapidly repel the energy).

He found that when a person, with their own energy field, "comes into contact with an accumulating device, the two fields make contact and excite each other, creating ... a strong orgonotic charge ... [that] may help strengthen the immune system, improve circulation and raise one's energy levels." [65]

Orgone energy, therefore, is an *inexpensive* way to help restore balance to the Earth.

---

[64]

http://orgonetachyondevices.loveomni.com/orgone%20information.ht ml

[65] Ibid.

Orgonite is an orgone energy transformer as well as an energy generator. Made of cured fiberglass resin, metal chips, copper coils and crystals, they have the ability to capture orgone energy and reverse its negative polarity, healing all living things within its vicinity.

Used by practitioners of Geomancy and Feng Shui, these devices have long been used for correcting energy imbalances. You can also avail of an orgone multipurpose disc (coaster style) [66] to orgonize and tachyonize your drinks.

Orgonite appears to manifest curious instances of synchronicity, and has a less than subtle way of showing how it works (making it very obvious). It has the ability to change, almost instantly, the atmosphere in work places as well as situations where there are high amounts of stress.

---

[66] Nathaniel Pitzer's website located at http://orgonetachyondevices.loveomni.com/oronge%20tachyon%20multi%20purpose%20disc%20.html

It is also able to transform electro smog, sick house syndrome, unwanted and invasive energies from pylons, communication towers, Tetra and Microwave, and any other unwanted negative energies.

In short, this simple, yet subtle technology, unknown by a great many, has the ability to improve the energetic quality of our environment.

Chi Generator® [67]

Etheric Warriors Forum [68]

Multi Purpose Orgone Disk [69]

Operation Paradise by Georg Ritschi [70]

Orgoknight (UK) [71]

---

[67] http://orgonetec.com/
[68] http://www.ethericwarriors.com/ip/viewtopic.php?p=4433
[69]
http://orgonetachyondevices.loveomni.com/oronge%20tachyon%20multi%20purpose%20disc%20.html
[70] http://www.lulu.com/product/paperback/operation-paradise-%28standard-edition-bw%29/2705804
[71] http://www.orgoknight.com/

Orgon 2010 (a site in French) [72]

Orgone Australia [73]

Orgone Energy Balancing (US) [74]

Orgone Products CT Busters (US) [75]

Orgone Pyramid and Crystal Harmonizer (US) [76]

Orgone (Tachyon) Pocket Devices [77]

Orgonise Africa [78]

Orgonite Information, Links and Resources [79]

---

[72] http://orgon2012.over-blog.com/
[73] http://www.orgoneaustralia.com.au/
[74] http://www.orgoneenergybalancing.org/index.html
[75] http://www.ctbusters.com/cart/orgoneproducts-c-22.html
[76]

http://www.worldwithoutparasites.com/Orgone_Pyramid_Crystal_Har
monizer.html
[77]

http://orgonetachyondevices.loveomni.com/orogone%20tachyon%20p
ocket%20devices%20.html
[78] http://www.orgoniseafrica.com/
[79] http://www.orgonite.info/

Orgonite Moksha (UK) [80]

Orgonite, Radionics and Life Force Technology [81]

Québec Orgone (Canada) [82]

Sea Orgonite (South East Asia) [83]

The Harmonic Protector (US) [84]

Ultimate Vision (US) [85]

Warrior Matrix Forum for Orgonite [86]

Whale Tactical and Practical Orgonite (UK) [87]

_____

[80] http://www.orgonitemoksha.co.uk/
[81] http://www.hscti.com/
[82] http://www.quebecorgone.com/catalog/index.php?language=en
[83] http://www.seaorgonite.com/
[84]
http://www.worldwithoutparasites.com/The_Harmonic_Protector.html
[85] http://ultimatevision.us/
[86] http://www.warriormatrix.com/
[87] http://www.whale.to/orgone/whaleorgone.htm

Psychic Awareness and Social Graces

Psychic awareness refers to both the understanding of human consciousness as well as the full potential of the mind, when applied to everyday life.

The meaning of the word "psyche" comes from Greek, translating as *the breath of life*. The word "psychic", also from Greek, means *of the soul, mental.* Psychic awareness, then, is literally a conscious comprehension of the *life force* or Spirit within us, and the power of the human mind. [88]

Psychic awareness simply means being more refined in your awareness, an important part of which entails learning how to listen to your own instincts. Psychic awareness also means trusting the decisions that you make.

As discussed in several of my books, You Are Everything: Everything Is You and The Awakening of Humanity: A Foremost Necessity, all is connected.

---

[88] http://www.metaphysics-for-life.com/psychic-awareness.html

In taking a more in-depth look at the discoveries in quantum physics, the Zero Point Field, and the effect of thought and emotion (on both our bodies as well as the environment), it is becoming more and more clear that our minds are not merely isolated biological machines that govern (and control) the workings of the bodily system.

The developing of psychic awareness is what gives us access to both the subconscious mind as well as the collective human consciousness. It is also a means with which to influence the energies that affect the totality of our very lives (including health, relationships, success).

It is my belief set that every living being is endowed with natural psychic abilities; and, yes, I did say *natural*. Unfortunately, over time, we have become more focused upon material things; likewise, we have also allowed ourselves to be heavily influenced by religion (what to believe, what to say, how to act).

In experiencing more and more scepticism along the way, however, these natural psychic abilities were forgotten and scoffed at (but never truly lost).

Once awakened, as with any ability, the more you use your psychic ability, the stronger it becomes. Psychic powers constitute such abilities as

[1] Clairvoyance (the ability to see beyond the physical world, often referred to as the Astral Plane)

[2] Clairaudience (the ability to hear people and other sounds from the Astral Plane and/or the afterlife)

[3] Clairsentience (the ability to feel and sense energies)

[4] Psychic Mediumship (the ability to make contact with deceased people)

[5] Psychic Intuition (the ability to sense and interpret psychic energy)

[6] Telepathy (the ability to communicate with another, using the medium of mind)

[7] Spirit Guides (the ability to communicate with your Spirit Guides)

[8] Higher Self (the ability to communicate with your Higher Self, for both guidance as well as answers)

[9] Psychometry (the ability to view or sense information through the holding of an object)

Brain Hemispheres [89]

Mind Over Matter [90]

Parapsychology [91]

Path of the Psychic [92]

Six Ways to Increase Your Psychic Awareness [93]

The Institute of Noetic Sciences [94]

---

[89] http://www.metaphysics-for-life.com/brain-hemispheres.html
[90] http://www.metaphysics-for-life.com/mind-over-matter.html
[91] http://www.metaphysics-for-life.com/parapsychology.html
[92] http://www.pathofthepsychic.com/
[93] http://www.awakening-intuition.com/IncreasePsychicAwareness.html
[94] http://noetic.org/research/participate/online-activities/

The Subconscious Mind [95]

The Universal Mind [96]

Thoughts Become Things [97]

In keeping with the Nine Pillars of Psychic Awareness, [98] as shared by Tana Hoy, [99] these components resonate with me as being what one might refer to as *pertinent social graces*; namely,

[1] Self-control: being able to shield one's self from the negative influence of others.

[2] Humility: the willingness to learn, the willingness to show understanding, striving for the well-being of others and contributing to the environment (by setting an admirable example).

---

[95] http://www.metaphysics-for-life.com/subconscious-mind.html
[96] http://www.metaphysics-for-life.com/universal-mind.html
[97] http://www.metaphysics-for-life.com/thoughts-become-things.html
[98] http://aurathirdeyepsychic.com/the-nine-pillars-of-psychic-awareness-a-psychic-ability-secret-revealed/
[99] http://tanahoy.com/

[3] Unconditional Love: psychic gifts should be used for the greater good, to help others, without expecting anything in return.

[4] Calmness and Focus: must be maintained in order to keep an open, concentrated, mind so one may connect with their inner psychic gift(s).

[5] Non-Attachment: detachment from material possessions allows for the pure intentions that are needed to fully unlock the true power of their ability.

[6] Intuition: learning to use your natural intuitive ability, while also trusting your instincts.

[7] Self Knowledge: no one knows you more than you know yourself; hence, it becomes through self knowledge that you can identify your strengths and weaknesses.

[8] Happiness: in order to fully hone the powers of your ability, you need to find true happiness (the kind of happiness that is synonymous with unchanging peacefulness and bliss; the kind of happiness that eludes one who finds themselves attached to material objects).

[9] Freedom: once you have mastered the previous eight pillars, you will enter into that state where your inner psychic is free to roam (meaning that your ability will be at full force).

Mediation, Diplomacy and Peacemaking

Mediation, a way in which to resolve disputes, between two or more parties, is a practice that was developed in ancient Greece. Roman law (circa 530 CE) also recognized mediation. In facilitative mediation, the mediator assists all parties in negotiating their own settlement. In evaluative mediation, where all parties agree, the mediator may express a view on what might be a fair or reasonable settlement. The mediation process is private and confidential, with the presence of a wholly impartial mediator being the distinguishing feature. [100]

Diplomacy references the art and practice of conducting negotiations between representatives of groups or states (as in international diplomacy). As such, diplomacy has been

---

[100] http://en.wikipedia.org/wiki/Mediation

practiced since the inception of civilization. In Europe, diplomacy began with the first city-states that were formed in ancient Greece. Diplomats (usually relatives of the ruling family and/or individuals possessing very high rank) were sent for specific negotiations, returning immediately after their mission concluded. [101]

Peacemaking is "essentially negotiation of an agreement formally ending a particular dispute ... followed by peace building which implements the agreement and brings the parties back together in some sort of *normal* relationship." [102]

Peacemakers can use diplomatic techniques, "such as facilitation, mediation, arbitration, and other measures to maintain and restore international peace and security. The United Nations mandates these under Chapters VI and VII of the UN Charter." [103]

---

[101] http://en.wikipedia.org/wiki/Diplomacy
[102]
http://www.colorado.edu/conflict/peace/!treating_core.htm#peacemkg
[103] http://www.international.gc.ca/peace-paix/making-retablissement.aspx?lang=en&view=d

Jedi Philosophy and Religion

Practitioners of Jediism, the religious movement based on the philosophical and spiritual ideas of the Jedi, as depicted in the Star Wars saga, believe in the existence of the Force. They also believe that interaction with the Force is possible. In aligning themselves with the moral code, as clearly demonstrated by the fictional Jedi, one Jedi church describes the religion as one that has incorporated beliefs from various religions, including Christianity, Buddhism, Taoism and Shintoism. [104]

While I am not a Jediist, I do adhere to many components affiliated with this religious movement; namely,

[1] I believe in the existence of a force that is identified by many names (energy field, quantum energy, an ocean of subatomic vibrations, Unified Field, Zero Point Field or ZPF, Divine Matrix, Consciousness, Consciousness Grid, Source of Creation, Oneness, Unity, Nature's Mind, Mind of God, Quantum Hologram, Maya and God).

---

[104] http://en.wikipedia.org/wiki/Jediism

Living the Jedi Way

[2] I believe, most strongly, that interaction with this force is possible, courtesy of thought creation (that which must exist before manifestation is achievable), be it positive or negative.

Positive thoughts beget freedom.

Negative thoughts beget bondage.

Positive thoughts result in inner balance and harmony, thereby healing the physical body.

Negative thoughts cause inner imbalance and disharmony, thereby creating disease in the body.

[3] I also adhere to the Buddhist philosophical beliefs, namely, the Four Noble Truths and the Noble Eightfold Path, which, in turn, aid in the liberation of the self. [105] [106]

---

[105] http://en.wikipedia.org/wiki/Four_Noble_Truths
[106] http://en.wikipedia.org/wiki/Noble_Eightfold_Path

[4] In keeping with the philosophy of Mahavira (the son of King Siddartha and Queen Trishala, Prince Vardhaman), I believe in nonviolence (causing no harm to any living being), truthfulness (speaking the harmless truth) and non-stealing (taking nothing not properly given). [107]

Teaching, Coaching and Mentoring

By definition, teaching can refer to [1] *the act, or profession, of a person who teaches*, [2] *something that is taught*, and [3] *doctrines or precepts* as in the teachings of Yeshua (Jesus).

In most cases, you are your own teacher; henceforth, spending time studying sacred texts (whatever books are relevant to you; whatever books inspire and teach you) is an important aspect of teaching, because education (the learning of something new) always changes (and enhances) one's perception (view) on knowledge, on life, on truth, on discernment, on enlightenment, on consciousness.

---

[107] http://en.wikipedia.org/wiki/Mahavira

In many cases, you will find yourself taking what resonates (at that point in your life) while leaving the rest behind.

You will also discover that in revisiting the same text, at some point in the future, you will be ready to acquire additional understanding from that which you previously had left behind.

By comparison, coaching means *to give instruction, or advice, in the capacity of a coach.*

Life coaching, for example, is a practice that helps people identify and achieve their personal goals, using a variety of tools and techniques (journaling, values assessment, behavior modification, behavior modeling, goal setting).

Bradley Thompson, president of the Advanced Life Coaching Institute, is also one of the world's best-selling self-help authors. [108] At present, I am working my way through this particular course.

---

[108] http://www.life-coaching-secrets.com/lifecoach/

In essence, life coaching involves learning how the subconscious mind works so that you (the client) may learn how to take control of your emotional state and behavior (through the reconfiguring of the subconscious mind); all of which serves to provide a positive and empowering approach to inner healing.

As you learn how to heal the past, you are able to change the negative beliefs that you have long held about yourself, the very means through which you are able to step out of victimhood and into your powerful authentic self.

Life coaching is about getting the very best out of someone and enabling them to make decisions that will improve their life.

In this way, life coaching "develops rather than imposes, and reflects rather than directs." [109]

Effective life coaching "is a form of change facilitation [that] is reactive and flexible, [allowing] for personal transition on an individual basis." [110]

---

[109] http://www.businessballs.com/lifecoaching.htm

Good personal coaching "seeks to help the other person's understanding of himself or herself," [111] wherein empathy is central to the overall process.

In addition, life coaching is an approach that "focuses on enablement and reflection, so that the individual decides and discovers their required progression themselves." [112]

Mentoring, while a possible approach to life coaching, on the other hand, means *to act as a mentor* wherein mentor references *a wise and trusted counselor or teacher*.

The focus of mentoring is to develop the whole person.

The most commonly used mentoring techniques are [113]

[1] Accompanying (making a commitment in a caring way, which involves taking part in the learning process side by side with the learner)

---

[110] http://www.businessballs.com/lifecoaching.htm
[111] Ibid.
[112] Ibid.
[113] http://en.wikipedia.org/wiki/Mentorship#Mentoring_techniques

[2] Sowing (mentors are often confronted with the difficulty of preparing the learner before he or she is ready to change, so sowing will be necessary when you know that what you say may not be understood or even acceptable to learners at first, but will make sense, and have value to the mentee, when the situation requires it)

[3] Catalyzing (when change reaches a critical level of pressure, the mentor chooses to plunge the learner right into change, provoking a different way of thinking, a change in identity or a re-ordering of values)

[4] Showing (this is making something understandable, or using your own example to demonstrate a skill or activity; you show what you are talking about, you demonstrate by your own behavior)

[5] Harvesting (here the mentor focuses creating an awareness of what was learned by experience so that conclusions may be drawn, with key questions being *What have you learned* and *How useful is this new knowledge*)

After careful reflection on these five techniques, I quickly came to realize that, as a Special Education teacher of 27 years, I have made use of them all, both instinctively, as well as intuitively, over the course of my career.

A Spiritual Teacher [114]

Heart Compass Life Navigation System [115]

What is the Role of a Spiritual Teacher or Mentor [116]

Defending and Protecting Others

While I applaud this aspect of Jedi training, it is my personal belief that *we are here to change ourselves* for the better.

As each individual changes things for themselves, so, too, does this mean changes for the whole (the macrocosm, the collective, the bigger picture).

---

[114] http://viewonbuddhism.org/spiritual_teacher_guru.html
[115] http://www.metaphysics-for-life.com/foundation-for-a-mind-with-heart.html
[116] http://endless-satsang.com/spiritual-teacher-mentor.htm

Objective Deliberation, Persuasion, and Debate

Deliberation pertains to giving something much careful consideration (which usually involves a lengthy discussion). In keeping, objective deliberation references consideration and discussion that is not influenced by personal feelings, judgments or biases; based on facts, objective deliberation is completely unbiased.

Persuasion, on the other hand, generally involves trying to convince someone else that *their* personal conviction(s) and/or belief(s) are correct.

Debating involves a formal discussion around opposing viewpoints.

Literary and Theatrical Arts

The Literary Arts generally refers to prose (fiction as well as non-fiction), drama and poetry.

The Theatrical Arts, by comparison, references what is known as the Performing Arts, most notably music, theatre and dance.

Individuals involved include writers, actors, comedians, dancers, musicians and singers.

Energy Work and the Supernatural

Everything is comprised of energy. Everything is vibration. All vibration is the result of energy in motion. Energy is held together to create matter. Matter is energy condensed to a slow vibration.

There is one underlying field of energy, the unified field (also referred to as the Zero Point Field or ZPF), that pervades everything, thereby giving purpose and unity to our world.

Everything in the universe has a unique vibrational energy. Every object, every being, every thought, every action, every psychological mood; in short, energy equals vibration.

The quality of your vibratory signature depends on both your thoughts and your inner mental (feeling) world.

If one feels inadequate, insecure and lacking in self esteem, this results in an inward withdrawal.

These individuals tend to become engulfed in a negative inner dialogue, one that is embodied by self-pity. It is this negative vibration that emanates outward.

In accordance with the Law of Attraction, this negative energy will only attract more of the same. No matter how much this person seeks happiness and success, in their life, they continue to feel more and more like a dismal failure, at anything and everything.

They may not understand that it is *one's inner world* that *must ultimately be changed before such can be duly reflected in the outer world* of which they are a part.

Focus and concentration are major keys with respect to the changing of one's inner world.

It is your energy vibration that attracts corresponding circumstances (be they people, places, things or events) into your life. By the same token, it is your energy vibration that can ultimately change your reality.

You are constantly projecting thought patterns.

If you are *conscious* of your thought patterns, then you are *creating by deliberate intent.*

If you are *unconscious* of your thought patterns, then you are *creating by default.*

The more you are able to remain open to a given experience, relaxing and embracing the situation at hand, doing your best to learn from the event itself, the easier it becomes to transcend, thereby allowing you to move beyond the experience in question.

Whatever you resist will persist, as the saying goes. It was Carl Jung who uttered these wise words.

He was a man who clearly understood that it is what you think about that recreates itself within your own life experience(s).

Negative energies, then, will only begin to dissipate in the welcoming, accepting and embracing of that which you want to change.

Most are familiar with the saying that *the outer world is your mirror*, always *reflecting yourself back to you*. This simply means that your outer world is a direct reflection of your inner world.

If you embrace and feel love, peace, unison and truth, vibrating such throughout the entirety of your being, you will experience people (as well as places, things or events) that emit these corresponding vibrations.

If, on the other hand, all you experience in your outer world is disharmony, aggression, hate, separation and falsehood, so, too, will you experience people (as well as places, things or events) that match these same resonance levels.

Much inner healing is needed in order to correct the imbalances that exist.

Accepting the premise that you, and you alone, are 100% responsible for the changes that you wish to impart upon your being, is also critical.

Living the Jedi Way

I am here to tell you that *it is possible to transcend situations in your outer world,* all *through the shifting of your inner terrain.*

However, this is not something that happens overnight. It is *a process that requires work, effort and diligence* on your part, of that you can be sure.

While it is not known to whom the following quote can be attributed, it is well worth citing herein.

The good you find in others, is within you as well. The faults you find in others, are your faults as well. After all, to recognize something in your outer world, you must have a reference point in your inner world. The world around you is a reflection, a mirror showing you the person you are. To change your world, simply change yourself. See the best in others, and you will be at your best. Give to others, and you give to yourself. Love others, and you will be loved. Seek to understand, and you will be understood. Listen, and your voice will be heard. Teach, and you will learn.

Working on yourself constitutes energy work. As well, please refer back to the mini section on Healing Arts (pages 34 to 54) as this also constitutes energy work.

It is also important to understand the differences that exist between two inter-related terms; namely, supernatural and paranormal.

Paranormal refers to experiences that lie outside the range of normal experience (as well as scientific explanation) whilst supernatural means that which is not subject to the laws of nature (as in crop circles, orbs, the mysteries of the Earth, UFOlogy, creatures, ghosts and spirits).

In the words of Albert Einstein, *the most beautiful thing we can experience is the mysterious.*

It is imperative that one be open-minded enough to acknowledge the mysterious.

Ghost PRO (Paranormal Research Organization) [117]

---

[117] http://www.ghostpro.org/

Omaha Research Beyond the Supernatural [118]

Paranormal and Supernatural [119]

Paranormal Research Society [120]

Paranormal Studies and Investigations Canada [121]

Supernatural Research Institute [122]

Supernatural Research Society [123]

The Paranormal Research Initiative [124]

Sustained Pursuit of Knowledge and Wisdom

Knowledge can be referred to as information gleaned from a multitude of sources: cognition; exoteric (which means communicated to the general public, as in familiar, known and evident).

---

[118] http://orbsomaha.com/default.htm
[119] http://www.qigongchinesehealth.com/psychic_abilities_research
[120] http://paranormalresearchsociety.org/
[121] http://psican.org/alpha/
[122] http://www.supernaturalresearch.com/
[123] http://www.srsocietync.webs.com/
[124] http://www.paranormalresearch.ca/

Wisdom, on the other hand, can be referenced as applied (lived) information: consciousness; esoteric (which means understood by, and meant for, a select few who have special knowledge or interest, as in hidden, mysterious, mystical and arcane).

Ardriana Cahill puts it thusly ... "Knowledge is but the messenger that calls you to wisdom, but it is not wisdom. One can gain knowledge, but one does not seek wisdom; one meets it when one often least expects it and recognizes it as kindred. Knowledge puts us in the way of wisdom, but wisdom is experiential; it is a truth one recognizes in the external world that already resides in the internal one. One cannot learn wisdom; one must awaken to it." [125]

Based on the comparative opening at the beginning of this chapter, knowledge is far more intellectual based when contrasted with wisdom, which, located within, is divine.

---

[125] *Knowledge versus Wisdom* article accessed on July 17, 2011 at http://www.controverscial.com/Knowledge%20vs%20Wisdom.htm

In the words of our brother, Yeshua ben Yosef, the one we have come to know as Jesus, "Seek ye knowledge and ye shall find the truth that liberates. Seek ye discipline in the persisting with positive thoughts. Seek ye the joy of creating, the joy of learning, the joy of experiencing. Seek ye the realm of infinite possibilities for therein ye shall find the all. Seek ye the seer that ye be." [126]

Would you define these words as knowledge or wisdom?

Clearly, the more you seek knowledge (all knowledge), the more wisdom you will experience.

Ardriana talks about the fact that knowledge and wisdom make use of two completely different organs when needing to communicate with you: "One is known, the other felt. The divine speaks to us through the spirit, not the mind. When wisdom is revealed to you (it does not explain itself), it reveals itself full blown, like manna from heaven on a silver platter. It awakens within as an all encompassing flood of warm illumination or a bolt of lightning that shocks

---

[126] Doucette, Michele. (2010) *Veracity At Its Best* (p 141). McMinnville, TN: St. Clair Publications.

or stuns you. This is why the sages call it enlightenment. Wisdom does not need digesting, deliberating, debating or dissecting by doubt or reason; it breathes within you as calm surety and perfect peace. It is then that you recognize [on an intellectual level], that this [inner knowing] has always been with you, just waiting for you to find it. From head to toe, you have everything you need to become extraordinary." [127]

The Vedas are a large body of texts, long preserved in ancient India, that constitute the oldest authority of Sanskrit literature. They are also the oldest Hindu scriptures.

While their exact date is controversial, it is quite possible that this knowledge dates back 10,000 years BC, meaning that they "were first written around 3,000 BC." [128]

The metaphysical foundation of Hinduism, as expressed in both the Vedas and the Upanishads, is "that reality (Brahman) is One or Absolute, changeless, perfect and

[127] *Knowledge versus Wisdom* article accessed on July 17, 2011 at http://www.controverscial.com/Knowledge%20vs%20Wisdom.htm
[128] *Ancient Eastern Philosophy* article accessed on July 17, 2011 at http://www.spaceandmotion.com/buddhism-hinduism-taoism-confucianism.htm

eternal. The ordinary human world of many separate and discrete (finite) things (which our mind represents by our senses) is an illusion. Through meditation and purity of mind, one can experience their true Self , which is Brahman, God, the One infinite eternal thing, which causes and connects the many things. True enlightenment is self-realisation, to experience the supreme reality as Self," [129] meaning that while you live, "you are the caretaker of the divine within you." [130]

It becomes through knowledge and wisdom that we are able to "eliminate fear, which produces understanding. We begin to understand who we are and why we are here. We recognize, with generosity, others stumbling, while seeking their way, and develop a keen awareness and love for the miracle that is all Life, and that includes oneself." [131]

---

[129] *Ancient Eastern Philosophy* article accessed on July 17, 2011 at http://www.spaceandmotion.com/buddhism-hinduism-taoism-confucianism.htm

[130] *Knowledge versus Wisdom* article accessed on July 17, 2011 at http://www.controverscial.com/Knowledge%20vs%20Wisdom.htm

[131] Ibid.

In essence, wisdom is a lifelong experience. While you must seek knowledge in order to reawaken wisdom, it soon becomes apparent that the more we know, the more we realize how much we don't know. Likewise, "the wiser we grow, the more wisdom we sense is yet to be discovered. With each step, we grow larger in each other's sight, we grow larger in the sight of the gods, and, it follows, the gods grow larger within us. Experiencing this knowledge, we find true humility and peace from the inside out." [132]

Knowledge changes over time.

Wisdom is timeless.

Knowledge, gathered from learning and education, is often referred to as one's intelligence. Wisdom is intuitive information (as in inner knowing, words that may come to you, visions and gut feelings). As such, wisdom is unlimited, coming together, courtesy of personal experience.

---

[132] *Knowledge versus Wisdom* article accessed on July 17, 2011 at http://www.controverscial.com/Knowledge%20vs%20Wisdom.htm

While knowledge (in the form of gathered data and pieces of information) does not exist merely to serve wisdom, given its correlation with lifelong experience, wisdom can be further enhanced through knowledge.

However, it seems to me as if each is connected on an even deeper level in that … *Knowledge becomes wisdom only after it has been put to practical use,* [133] thereby requiring active participation and action.

Mind you, without wisdom, knowledge can become dangerous, leading to conceit and selfishness.

This is why it becomes essential to "use your intellect and your cognitive processes, as well as the wisdom that comes from your intuitive knowledge. The combination of these aspects is a powerful one, and will show you the truth that is right for you." [134]

---

[133] http://www.indiadivine.org/audarya/advaita-vedanta/142414-some-quotes-knowledge-wisdom.html

[134] Bendriss, Lilli and Løken, Camillo. (2011) *The Shift in Consciousness* (p. 13). Milton Keynes, UK: Lightning Source UK Ltd.

In most cases, it will be your heart leading the way.

You are both co-creator, as well as creation, of this vast, majestic, infinite universe.

Everything is created within your own consciousness.

Everything created by you first existed in thought, followed by feeling. Knowing that thought, then, materializes into your external reality, it becomes important to become increasingly aware of what you are thinking.

Most people are *enslaved by their thoughts*, thereby *creating by default* (creation by way of an unconscious means).

It simply does not occur to them that they can free themselves from the chatter of the mind.

There can be no peace of mind, no stillness, when one is engulfed by negativity, and, yet, inner peace is within reach of each and every individual.

Therein lies the juxtaposition, if you will.

85

When the mind is silent, happiness reigns inside and out. It is to one's advantage, therefore, to be able to still the incessant and compulsive chatter of the mind.

The majority are so deeply ingrained within the confines of the human race, that they often defer their thinking to someone other than themselves.

Everyday life, for the multitude, seems to be fraught with worry, tension, anxiety and fear.

Thoughts easily arise, in the mind, that also serve to reflect these same outer feelings.

In order to break free (so as to regain control of your own mind), you must first become aware of the problem. Thereafter, you must work, consciously and diligently, toward reconfiguring how you think, how you respond, how you act.

The source of all thought is, of course, the conscious mind; the part of us that deals with logic, reasoning (inductive, deductive, analytic and synthetic) and judgment.

The source of all power, on the other hand, is the subconscious mind; the part of us that deals with intuition, emotion, inspiration, memory and imagination.

You must learn to *think only about what you want*, accepting it as part of your life.

It is also imperative that you achieve vibrational harmony with what you are creating.

You will know that you have achieved, and/or are achieving, alignment with your thought(s) when you feel happy, contented, elated, peaceful, ecstatic, overjoyed, playful and upbeat. The deeper the feeling(s) experienced, the closer the alignment.

The power of expectation is crucial, for expectation is intention; likewise, thought is also intention.

If "you desire one thing while expecting another, you are sending out two intentions that conflict and oppose each other; to be completely intentional, it means you [must] think about your desire and expect it to happen. Having all your thoughts in alignment with a single direction will ensure that your desire manifests without complications." [135]

Knowing what you want gives you the clarity that is needed.

Repetition of a chant, a mantra, an affirmation ... all leads to belief. As soon as the belief has become instilled as a deep conviction, things begin to happen. Therein lies the psychology, and power, of repeated suggestion (which can also be used wrongly, so please be careful in this respect).

Fearful thoughts create fearful situations and hard times. By direct association, when all of the citizens of this planet stop thinking about war and destruction, so, too, will these perils cease to exist.

We create by way of our emotional thinking.

Thought is the greatest force in the world, and, as stated earlier, *everything begins with thought*. Whatever you fix your thought(s) upon (meaning whatever you steadily fix your imagination on) is what you shall attract.

---

[135] Tan, Enoch. *Power of Expectation* article (August 2008).

It is imperative that you work to keep your dynamic vision alive, without being swayed by what you read, by what you see, by what you hear. Pictures (as in vision boards) can be most instrumental; the more often you visualize your desire, the faster its manifestation shall be.

It is a known scientific fact that, relative to quantum cohabitation, two atoms (mass) cannot occupy the same quantum space simultaneously. This is referred to as the Pauli-Einstein principle.

If you keep your mind filled with positive, creative and powerful thoughts, there will be little space left for that which is negative (fearful, doubtful and troublesome).

You must decide which thoughts shall continue to reside within your own mind.

As individuals think and believe, this is what they become. Every person is an image of their own thinking and believing.

It must also be reiterated that the subconscious mind will automatically respond to the thoughts that dominate.

Unless you successfully close your mind to negative thoughts, immediately counteracting them with positive ones, sooner or later even the most powerful will succumb to the destructive effects of these detrimental thoughts.

A mental picture is the same thing as a thought projection; just envision the movie projectors of old in order to achieve an operable visual. If these thought projections remain steadfast and unwavering, it is with consistent practice and concentrated effort that you achieve that which you desire, all courtesy of the subconscious mind.

In short, you become energized action in motion.

The more interest you take in any initiative, the more attention and energy you naturally give.

Knowing that energy follows thought, it only makes sense that you continue to experience greater results in keeping with said initiative; the more absorbing the initiative, the better.

Possessing the right mental attitude, in combination with remaining firmly fixed on that which is your steadfast goal, is what creates the necessary ambiance to achieve.

Interestingly, it actually becomes through the cooperation of both the conscious mind, together with the subconscious mind, that you can succeed.

You must believe (earnestly, sincerely, strongly and completely), for it is belief that makes things happen.

Knowing that many continue to be controlled by way of collective (mass) thinking, true happiness, as sought by many, has always been actualized by so few.

Located within, happiness is a state of mind that we, ourselves, have the power to control.

When you come to know yourself (completely and in all ways) while also taking full ownership and responsibility for that which you create, you will also come to know (and wholeheartedly embrace) the power of thought.

Just take the time to think about using your power to develop a healthy, caring and open minded outlook towards the interconnectedness of life (demonstrating empathy for others, demonstrating an important life purpose, seeking a balance between work, play, creativity and spirituality); all of which serves to create a healthy body.

Most have experienced that special, almost magical, moment in which everything seems perfect.

Each time I hold a sleeping newborn, I am able to feel the completeness, wholeness, and perfection, of life. I also experience these same feelings when held, in a warm embrace, by someone who loves me.

When I am engaged in a writing project, one that requires extensive research as well as personal reflection, so, too, am I able to tap into these same, wondrous, energies.

These are the moments of oneness with creation. You feel a sense of rightness, a sense of innate goodness.

These are the very moments that restore us spiritually.

These are the very moments that recharge us emotionally.

These are the very moments that do wonders for us on a physical level, making us feel more vibrant and alive.

You have the power to experience these moments each day, should that be your wish.

Living in the now refers to living in the moment. Living in the moment is also called mindfulness. In truth, nothing exists outside of this present moment.

As you become mindful of your thoughts, words, emotions, feelings and actions, you are learning to be fully present in the moment.

Whenever I find myself stressed, worried, angry or anxious, I stop what I am doing. I simply close my eyes and breathe.

Taking a deep breath, I hold it for a count of ten before slowing exhaling. I take the time to continue breathing, in this same manner, for several moments.

Many are controlled by their thoughts of stress, worry and anger. In order to feel more in control, you need to step out of, and learn to detach yourself from that mode of existence, otherwise you shall never be able to locate the necessary pause in keeping with the now.

In coming to grips with the fact that you are not your thoughts, you eventually learn to become an observer of your thoughts (emotions, feelings) from moment to moment, without judging them.

You are here to awaken to experience.

You are here to live fully and completely.

You are here to enjoy life.

You are here to experience inner freedom.

You are here to live a life of empowerment.

If you are to experience anything in life, you must create it in the present moment because unless it exists in some form, in the here and now, it will not exist at all.

What is it, then, that you wish to create?

How do you feel about your life in this very moment?

There is a considerable difference between creating freedom, peace, love, joy and wealth as compared to creating confinement, war, hatred, obligation and scarcity.

All that you wish for in the future (which refers to tomorrow) must be seeded in the here and now.

In the words of Andrew Cohen, editor of EnlightenNext Magazine ... *Spiritual development, as I understand it, is about compelling ourselves, through the power of our own inspired will and intention, to actually evolve. And in order to evolve, to consciously evolve, you first need to get to know the multidimensional nature of who you are and how you are.*

You need to be able to recognize and understand what constitutes your interior world — the infinite nature of the spiritual ground of your own being, the higher human capacities that make conscious evolution possible, and also the unconscious conditioned structures that can obstruct and obscure that potential.

You need to examine the fundamental dimensions of the self, both relative and absolute; understand the unique challenges and potentials of the cultural context in which we find ourselves; and cultivate those higher human capacities that can enable you to participate in such a bold and significant task as the evolution of the interior of the cosmos.

Like a great many held captive to their thoughts, to their feelings, to their emotions, I did not always live in the present moment.

I was so controlled by them that I was drowning in sorrow, depression, anxiety, worry and frustration. Instead of living, I was merely existing; there is little joy to be found within that life choice.

You are not here to change anyone other than yourself. Translated another way, this means that you are here to live your own life.

How, then, must one live in order to make that much needed connection to the now?

[1] Take the time to reconnect with nature. Take the time to pay close attention to the sights, sounds, smells and textures (as in walking barefoot on both the dewy grass as well as the warm sand) that instantly rise up to greet you.

[2] Take the time to savour your food, enjoying their colors, textures, smells and taste combinations.

[3] Begin each day with the same routine (by greeting the sun as it rises high in the skyline; by engaging in meditation; by engaging in some form of exercise; by watching your Mind Movie; by perusing your vision board), unique to you and your needs.

[4] Engage in activities that both interest and excite you, fueling you with much needed energy (which also translates to living your bliss). Take the time to do the things that you love.

[5] Stop playing video games in order to better engage your mind (books, crossword puzzles, movies).

[6] Take the time to focus on the things that really matter.

[7] Learn to become more positive (through identifying negative thoughts and mindsets and then reconfiguring them) each and every day.

[8] Take the time to feel the pain of suffering (as it comes your way) and then move forward, fully embracing all of the good that life has to offer.

[9] Take the time to truly understand the life of another (preferably someone living in conditions that are less than your own).

[10] Engage in play activities with children. More than anyone else, children know how to live in the moment. Take the time to relearn how to be joyful in your play with children and with each other.

[11] Recognize the importance of experiencing wisdom when you speak with your elders.

[12] Take the time to learn something new, to experience something that you have always wanted to experience.

[13] Rediscover your own spirituality.

[14] Take the time to learn to be still (while also relishing the stillness) by reading, sitting in the warm sun (and appreciating the warmth) or taking a nap.

[15] Stop watching the news on TV in order to learn to think for yourself, in order to learn to approach life from both a heart-based consciousness as well as a positive mindset.

[16] Rediscover comedy in all of its glorious forms; in truth, laughter is the best medicine.

In the words of Babatunde Olatunji ... *Yesterday is history. Tomorrow is a mystery. Today is a gift. That's why we call it ... the present.*

In a personal email (dated September 23, 2011) entitled *Welcome to Jedi Training*, author Elizabeth Trutwin shares that "thousands of years ago, Starfleet Academy began offerings to the Ground Crew on Earth called Jedi Training. These evolved humans, ascended masters, sages and Masters knew a darker time would come to Earth and humans would need these teachings to help them remember who they are."

While the following principles are universal principles, meaning that they are owned by all, Elizabeth also shares that ......

[1] Jedi Training contains all that is needed for the total unfoldment of human potential.

[2] Jedi Training teaches unity, integrity, balance and attunement to the Force.

[3] Jedi Training is the blueprint for evolution.

[4] Jedi Training teaches a method of growth based on physical fitness, mental profoundness and Self-realization.

[5] When the Jedi grows, all life grows.

[6] The Force respects all cultures, creeds and nations. This in turn nurtures the higher aspects of humanity, cooperation, compassion and peace.

[7] In Jedi Training, learning comes from a teacher.

One teacher of note sums up Jedi Training this way ... "We believe in One All-Pervading, Infinite Divinity [The Force] which resides in all of Creation and beyond all limitations, and is especially manifest in the hearts of all [Jedis]. That this [Master Teacher] inspires within seekers sincerity, love, wisdom and joy. That all bodies are temples for the Holy Spirit, and that the duty of man is to honor God through respect to all beings of creation, and attentive devotion in the pursuit of Self-realization." [136]

In keeping, there are no limitations in applying oneself to Jedi Training. Likewise, there are no age requirements, no physical requirements; all are welcome; all are needed in every vocation to serve humanity.

As one Master Teacher puts it ... "Diseases which affect the mind are the first and are not the easiest to heal; those which affect the body may be classed as secondary. The desires which affect the mind are primary diseases; we have sunk thus far by absence of Wisdom, and lack of Mastery over

---

[136] Trutwin, Elizabeth. *Welcome to Jedi Training* email dated September 23, 2011.

ourselves. We are under the seeming power of delusion. We cannot realize to what extent we are pulled down by such delusion. The mental disease is similar to the coming of a winter storm. When the power of desires gets hold of one, he then is liable to be guilty of fearful [action]; this in turn produces bodily disease. Bodily disease is also brought on by overeating, living in unhealthy places, association with impure desires, evil thoughts, etc. These mental or indirect diseases have a direct effect upon the body." [137]

Elizabeth Trutwin has written a book entitled Sacred Galactic Scripture Vaimanika Shastra: Starseeds' Jedi Training that explores the lessons that are involved, and tests that are required, for Jedi Training may begin at any time and on any level. [138] The only thing that is required, she says, is a sincere open heart and devotion to learning from the teacher.

When the Student is ready, the Master appears is a well known Buddhist proverb.

---

[137] Trutwin, Elizabeth. *Welcome to Jedi Training* email dated September 23, 2011.
[138] http://www.amazon.com/dp/0615506593/

The biggest hurdle in Jedi Training is mastery over one's self, which also involves purifying the *diseases of the mind* such as egoic thought, worry, depression, anger, doubt and envy. In retrospect, they can also be considered mental imbalances.

While it may seem simple, dissolving ego can be very difficult.

As these diseases are cured and one moves along on their training, the next step is acquiring the consciousness of absolute purity.

How, then, does one enter Jedi Training?

[1] Go deep inside your heart.

[2] Connect with the Inner Teacher, your Highest Self and with sincerity ask to have your teacher brought to you.

This is where you begin, by making a commitment on the inner level.

[3] The next step is to pursue unselfish action in all that you do.

[4] Engage ceaselessly in inquiring, for that is how you will find the real, the reality, which is the means to mastery over one's self.

While Elizabeth Trutwin also shares that there are eight primary skills (Jedi Knight) and ten advanced skills (Jedi Master), the Jedi's highest responsibility must become focused on both inner discipline as well as how they treat their own Highest Self. [139]

She also talks about ......

[1] Purity: meaning that you are to keep yourself, your clothing, and your surroundings clean. You also must partake of fresh and healthy food.

[2] Contentment: meaning that you must learn to cultivate contentment and tranquility by finding happiness with what you have and who you are. You are here to seek happiness in the moment, take responsibility for where you are, and choose to grow from there.

---

[139] Trutwin, Elizabeth. *Welcome to Jedi Training* email dated September 23, 2011.

[3] Austerity: meaning that you must also learn to show discipline in body, speech, and mind. The purpose of developing self-discipline, in this manner, is not to become ascetic, but to control and direct the mind and body for Jedi Training.

[4] Study: meaning that you will need to spend time studying sacred texts (whatever books are relevant to you; whatever books inspire and teach you) because education changes a person's outlook.

[5] Living with an awareness of the Divine: in that you are devoted to the Force. [140]

---

[140] Trutwin, Elizabeth. *Welcome to Jedi Training* email dated September 23, 2011.

The Jedi Code of Ethics

Researching this aspect of the book has been most interesting.

The Jedi Code [141] as presented in literature, and represented in five segments, states that ...

[1] There is no emotion; there is peace.

[2] There is no ignorance; there is knowledge.

[3] There is no passion; there is serenity.

[4] There is no chaos; there is harmony.

[5] There is no death; there is the Force.

141

http://templeofthejediforce.org/modules/newbb/viewtopic.php?topic_id=6&forum=2

106

The Jedi Goals, [142] in continuation of the same ...

[1] <u>The Goal of Peace</u>: Jedi work for peace, both within and without.

While we are all human, and all have emotions, we use meditation and study to know when we are working from a basis of emotion, and when we are working from a basis of right action.

[2] <u>The Goal of Knowledge</u>: Particularly when combined with the previous goal, this makes the Jedi sound as if they are heartless, emotionless, calculating machines. Nothing could be further from the truth.

The Jedi trusts in the Force, but the Force helps those who first help themselves.

A Jedi seeks to know all that is knowable, and to apply that knowledge in any situation.

142

http://templeofthejediforce.org/modules/newbb/viewtopic.php?topic_i d=6&forum=2

Instead of acting from [uncontrolled] emotion, the Jedi acts from knowledge, with humility.

[3] The Goal of Serenity: This is, in a way, a repeated injunction against acting from a basis of emotion, before knowledge is achieved.

Everyone has strong feelings, but the Jedi learns to take a step back from any situation in which strong feelings are impelling him or her towards precipitous action, taking the time to consider what the right action is, instead.

[4] The Goal of Harmony: The Jedi seeks harmony, both within and without.

If a Jedi feels chaos within, it is hard to work for harmony without.

If a Jedi is calm and at harmony, as is apparent in their actions, such spreads to those around them. Jedi seek to build communities.

The Duties of the Jedi [143] (as proceeding from the goals inherent within the code) ...

[1] The Duty of Discipline: Richard Bach wrote that the only true discipline is self-discipline.

It is not when we see the Jedi Code as an imposition that we succeed in being Jedi, but when we accept it as the ideal to which to aspire.

It is not when we see meditation as an imposition on our time that we perform it, but when we see it as a joy.

We cannot set aside the reactions our emotions propel us toward, if we are not disciplined in our selves.

We cannot disregard the promptings of passion, if we have not built our will to do so.

We cannot acquire knowledge, if we have not studied.

143

http://templeofthejediforce.org/modules/newbb/viewtopic.php?topic_i
d=6&forum=2

By means of discipline, we can set aside overconfidence, and have a true knowledge of our own capabilities.

By means of discipline, we can set aside defeatism, and know that we can accomplish.

By means of discipline, we can set aside arrogance, set aside stubbornness, set aside all that stands between us and accomplishing good in the world.

[2] The Duty of Responsibility: When we have accepted discipline, we can accept responsibility.

All Jedi must accept responsibility for their own actions.

When we have approached a situation without aggression and with knowledge, we may act rightly.

Sometimes, even right action has unforeseen consequences.

The Jedi accepts responsibility for the consequences of all action, and endeavors to set things right.

This does not mean that the Jedi, fueled by a belief in what is right, may disregard laws. Jedi are not above the law.

If a situation means that the Jedi must break the law, one of the consequences of that action is facing the penalty imposed by the law; this is taking responsibility for one's actions.

It is far more responsible to work within the law, to resolve injustice, than to break the law.

It is far more responsible to create harmony, than to create discord.

The Jedi seeks to create community; within community, each cares for the other.

[3] The Duty of Service: Jedi defend the defenseless, help the helpless, and bring hope to the hopeless.

This is service to others, and service to the self.

This does not mean that the Jedi must be a super-human.

Help may be rendered on many scales, and the Jedi must select the scale which is appropriate to the situation and to the means of the Jedi.

When we stop to help another change a tire on the road, this is service.

When we contact the news media to report injustice, this is service.

Though the popular conception of the Jedi is of the knight with lit lightsabre, the knight who must ignite the sabre has failed.

It is more responsible to build than to destroy; more disciplined to accept that the direct path may not be the correct path.

A Jedi is a mediator, building harmony between opposing sides.

A Jedi does not seek to impose a solution, but to build one by consensus.

At the most basic level, the Jedi Code [144] offers an important set of guidelines to follow.

Consider the first rule ... *There is no emotion; there is peace.*

It is plainly a contrast, distinguishing the confusion of emotional considerations from the clear thinking of peaceful meditation (a valuable quality). If that peace is rooted in simply being unaware of some factor that would otherwise cause a Jedi to feel an emotional reaction, then it is not so much peace as ignorance.

This is why the Code contains the second rule ... *There is no ignorance; there is knowledge.*

This teaches the Jedi to strive for understanding of all situations, particularly before acting, to better avoid errors in judgment. But, again, knowing a thing well can lead one to become engrossed in it. Likewise, engrossment often leads to the clouding of the mind.

---

[144] http://www.communigate.co.uk/ne/earthjedi2/page5.phtml

Thus, the third rule ... *There is no passion; there is serenity.*

Knowing a thing objectively, is knowing it as the Force knows it. Still, students commonly argue that the only true objectivity is non-existence (death). For does one not affect something in the course of merely observing it?

This is why there is the fourth rule ... *There is no death; there is the Force.*

The Force knows all things objectively, it is serene, and it is not swayed by emotion. Thus, the Jedi Code teaches that before undertaking any action, the Jedi should consider the will of the Force. In fact, it was Master Odan-Urr who said that "with these other considerations aside, all that remains is the Force." [145] What he meant by this was that if a Jedi can act emotionlessly, knowledgeably, and serenely, then they are acting in accordance with the will of the Force.

145

http://templeofthejediforce.org/modules/newbb/viewtopic.php?topic_i d=6&forum=2

If a Jedi, therefore, acts in all things without emotion, ignorance, or passion, then that Jedi is truly a Master of the Force.

Peace over anger; honor over hate; strength over fear.

It was later that I discovered a response to the previous website posting about the Jedi Code.

I would agree with most of your last post, except for a few points. I believe it is nearly impossible to eradicate emotion that we, as humans, and Jedi even more so, try to purge ourselves of.

However, I would not want to purge myself of the most beautiful and most powerful emotion of all ... Love; this emotion transcends existence with a power that cannot be described.

As for your short phrases at the bottom, I think they should be changed somewhat to:

Peace over anger; <u>love</u> over hate; <u>hope</u> over fear. [146]

Taoism

Taoism (also spelled as Daoism) refers to a philosophical tradition in which the basic concept is to establish harmony with the Tao, which is both everything that exists, as well as the origin of everything and nothing. The word Tao (or Dao, pronounced Dow) is usually translated as *way*, *path* or *principle* to happiness. [147] In retrospect, when you look at life, while also thinking about things, in the right way, you will find that you are much happier.

The <u>Tao Te Ching</u>, "written in China roughly 2,500 years ago (at about the same time when Buddha expounded the Dharma in India and Pythagoras taught in Greece), provides the basis for the philosophical school of Taoism, which is an important pillar of Chinese thought. Taoism teaches that there is one undivided truth at the root of all things." [148]

---

[147] http://en.wikipedia.org/wiki/Taoism
[148] http://www.thebigview.com/tao-te-ching/

365 Tao Daily Meditations [149]

About Taoism [150]

Accurate Translation of the Tao Te Ching [151]

An Introduction to Taoism [152]

Center of Traditional Taoist Studies [153]

Confucianism and Taoism [154]

Daoist Philosophy [155]

Lao Tzu and Taoism [156]

Power Point Presentations on Taoism [157]

149

http://www.harpercollins.com/browseinside/index.aspx?isbn13=97800
62502230
[150] http://taoism.about.com/
[151] http://www.taoism.net/ttc/complete.htm
[152] http://urantiabook.org/archive/readers/601_taoism.htm
[153] http://www.tao.org/
[154] http://religions.mrdonn.org/taoism.html
[155] http://www.iep.utm.edu/daoism/
[156] http://www.taoisminfo.com/
[157] http://religions.mrdonn.org/powerpoints/taoism.html

Taoism [158]

Taoism [159]

Taoism [160]

Taoism [161]

Taoism [162]

Taoism 101: Introduction to the Tao [163]

Taoism: Ageless Wisdom for a Modern World [164]

Taoism and the Philosophy of Tai Chi Chuan [165]

Taoism and the Taoist Arts [166]

---

[158] http://www.religioustolerance.org/taoism.htm
[159] http://www.beliefnet.com/Faiths/Taoism/index.aspx
[160] http://www.goldenelixir.com/taoism.html
[161] http://www.bbc.co.uk/religion/religions/taoism/
[162] http://www.diversitywatch.ryerson.ca/backgrounds/taoism.htm
[163] http://personaltao.com/taoism-library/articles/taoism-101/
[164] http://www.jadedragon.com/tao_heal/lao_tzu1.html
[165] http://www.chebucto.ns.ca/Philosophy/Taichi/taoism.html
[166] http://www.taoistarts.net/

Taoism: A Portrait [167]

Taoism Canada [168]

Taoism Directory [169]

Taoism Initiation Page [170]

Taoism Virtual Library [171]

Taoist Philosophy [172]

Taoist Sacred Texts [173]

Tao Te Ching by Lao Tzu [174]

The Art of Tai Chi [175]

---

[167] http://origin.org/ucs/sbcr/taoism.cfm
[168] http://www.taoismcanada.com/
[169] http://www.taoism-directory.org/
[170] http://www.taopage.org/
[171] http://www.vl-site.org/taoism/index.html
[172] http://people.howstuffworks.com/taoist-philosophy.htm
[173] http://www.sacred-texts.com/tao/index.htm
[174] http://www.thebigview.com/tao-te-ching/
[175] http://www.taoist.org/

The Tao of Star Wars [176]

The Three Teachings [177]

True Tao Home Page [178]

What Do Taoists Believe? [179]

---

[176] http://www.beliefnet.com/Faiths/Taoism/The-Tao-Of-Star-Wars.aspx
[177] http://ancienthistory.mrdonn.org/3Teachings.html
[178] http://www.taoism.net/enter.htm
[179] http://www.beliefnet.com/Faiths/Taoism/What-Do-Taoists-Believe.aspx

Zen Buddhism

Zen is a school of Mahāyāna Buddhism. The word Zen is from the Japanese pronunciation of the Chinese word Chán, which in turn is derived from the Sanskrit word dhyāna, which can be approximately translated as *meditation* or *meditative state.* [180]

Zen emphasizes experiential wisdom in the attainment of enlightenment, meaning that it de-emphasizes theoretical knowledge in favor of direct self-realization (through meditation and dharma practice). [181]

The emergence of Zen, as a distinct school of Buddhism, was first documented in China in the 7th century CE. [182]

Zazen constitutes the heart of Zen practice. It is through "right practice of Zazen that our expectation mind is not followed; it is our expectation mind that is not content with

---

[180] http://en.wikipedia.org/wiki/Zen_buddhism
[181] Ibid.
[182] Ibid.

the way things are, and it is the habitual act of following our expectation mind which is precisely what makes us not accept the very basic pervasive beauty which our life actually is." [183]

The unnecessary mystery of Zen, therefore, revolves around the understanding that life is always pure, despite our own expectations.

About Zen [184]

Buddha [185]

Buddhism Games and Activities for Children [186]

How to Begin Zen Meditation (Zazen) [187]

Japanese Zen Buddhist Philosophy [188]

---

[183] http://www.maximumbliss.com/zen%20meditation.asp
[184] http://zen.thetao.info/
[185] http://www.iep.utm.edu/buddha/
[186] http://www.wartgames.com/themes/religions/buddhism.html
[187] http://www.wikihow.com/Begin-Zen-Meditation-(Zazen)
[188] http://plato.stanford.edu/entries/japanese-zen/

Osho on Zazen Meditation [189]

Power Point presentations on Buddhism [190]

Satori in Zen Buddhism [191]

Shambhala Sun [192]

Steve Jobs' Mantra Rooted in Buddhism [193]

The Paradoxical Spiritual Materialist Buddhist [194]

The Zen Site [195]

Zazen [196]

---

[189] http://www.oshoteachings.com/osho-on-zazen-meditation-zazen-means-just-sitting/
[190] http://religions.mrdonn.org/powerpoints/buddhism.html
[191] http://sped2work.tripod.com/satori.html
[192] http://www.shambhalasun.com/index.php?option=content&task=view&id=29&Itemid=161
[193] http://news.yahoo.com/steve-jobs-mantra-rooted-buddhism-focus-simplicity-161250480.html
[194] http://therandomfact.com/ansteve-jobs-the-paradoxical-spiritual-materialist-buddhist/2210391/
[195] http://www.thezensite.com/
[196] http://www.dharma-rain.org/zazen/whatis.html

Zazen [197]

Zazen Meditation Guide [198]

Zazen Sitting Postures [199]

Zen 101: An Introduction to Zen Buddhism [200]

Zen as Buddhism [201]

Zen Buddhism [202]

Zen Buddhism [203]

Zen, Buddhism and Personality [204]

Zen Buddhism: Sacred Texts [205]

---

[197] http://the-wanderling.com/zazen.html
[198]
http://www.zenguide.com/zenmedia/books/chapters.cfm?t=zazen_med
itation_guide
[199] http://www.bisbeelotussangha.org/sittingpostures.htm
[200] http://buddhism.about.com/od/chanandzenbuddhism/a/zen101.htm
[201] http://www.katinkahesselink.net/tibet/zen-buddhism.html
[202] http://www.metmuseum.org/toah/hd/zen/hd_zen.htm
[203] http://www.magma.ca/~yeti/bu.html
[204] http://homepages.rpi.edu/~verwyc/Zen.htm
[205] http://www.sacred-texts.com/bud/zen/

Zen Buddhism Websites [206]

Zen Buddhism: Zen Enlightenment [207]

Zen Elephant [208]

Zen for Beginners [209]

Zen Guide [210]

Zen History [211]

Zazen: The Art of Doing Nothing [212]

Zen: The Path of Meditation [213]

---

[206] http://www.buddhanet.net/l_zen.htm
[207] http://the-wanderling.com/zen_enlightenment5.html
[208] http://www.totemdog.com/zen/
[209] http://webdharma.com/ctzg/zenforbeginners.html
[210]

http://www.zenguide.com/principles/zen_buddhism_dictionary_glossa
ry_terms.cfm
[211] http://www.karate.butsu.net/onzen/zen_history.html
[212] http://www.meditationrocks.us/zazen-easiest-meditation-the-art-of-
doing-nothing
[213] http://www.religionfacts.com/buddhism/sects/zen.htm

Zen: The Quest for Truth [214]

Qigong

Qigong (pronounced chee-gong) is a practice of aligning breath, movement and awareness for exercise, healing and meditation. With roots in Chinese medicine, martial arts and philosophy, Qigong is traditionally viewed as a practice to balance *chi* (intrinsic life energy). From a philosophical and spiritual perspective, Qigong is believed to help develop human potential and to awaken one to their true nature. [215]

Physical training is required if one is to become a Jedi Knight. Both Qigong, as well as Tai Chi, may comprise one's physical training in this aspect.

A Comprehensive Review of Health Benefits of Qigong and Tai Chi [216]

---

[215] http://en.wikipedia.org/wiki/Qigong

[216]

http://www.ncbi.nlm.nih.gov/pmc/articles/PMC3085832/?tool=pubmed

A Discourse on Qigong and Medicine [217]

Anti-Aging Benefits of Qigong [218]

Benefits of Qigong [219]

CFQ Healing Qigong Society of Atlantic Canada [220]

East West Academy of Healing Arts (Dr. Effie Chow) [221]

Health Benefits of Qigong Healing [222]

Health Benefits of Tai Chi and Qigong [223]

LAMAS Qi Gong Association of Canada [224]

---

[217] http://www.qi-journal.com/Qigong.asp?Name=A Discourse on Qigong and Medicine&-token.D=Article

[218] http://www.qigonginstitute.org/html/papers/Anti-Aging_Benefits_of_Qigong.html

[219] http://taoism.about.com/od/qigongchinesemedicine/p/benefits.htm

[220] http://www.cfqatlantic.ca/index.htm

[221] http://www.eastwestqi.com/

[222] http://www.learningstrategies.com/Qigong/Intro3.asp

[223] http://www.webmd.com/balance/health-benefits-tai-chi-qigong

[224] http://www.lamasqigongcanada.com/

Multifaceted Health Benefits of Medical Qigong [225]

Qigong Institute [226]

Qi Gong Live [227]

Qigong Master Projecting His Chi Energy [228]

Qigong Research and Practice Center [229]

Qi: The Journal of Traditional Eastern Health and Fitness [230]

Research Into Qigong Psychic Abilities [231]

Shou-Yu Liang Wushu Taiji Qigong Institute [232]

Spring Forest Qigong [233]

---

[225]

http://www.qigonginstitute.org/html/papers/Multifaceted_Benefits_Medical_Qigong.pdf
[226] http://www.qigonginstitute.org/main_page/main_page.php
[227] http://www.qigonglive.com/
[228] http://www.youtube.com/watch?v=nu99GRUUN6Y
[229] http://www.qigonghealing.com/qigong/index.html
[230] http://www.qi-journal.com/index.asp
[231] http://www.qigongchinesehealth.com/psychic_abilities_research
[232] http://www.shouyuliang.com/index.shtml
[233] http://www.bornahealer.com/

Spring Forest Qigong [234]

Tai Chi and Meditation Centre [235]

The Origins of Qi Gong [236]

Wu & Yeung® Qi Gong Wellness Institute [237]

Yan Xin Qigong ® [238]

Zhong Yuan Qigong Association of Canada [239]

---

[234] http://www.learningstrategies.com/Qigong/home.asp
[235] http://www.torontotaichimeditationcentre.com/index.html
[236] http://literati-tradition.com/qi_gong_origins.html
[237] http://www.masterteresa.com/
[238] http://yanxinqigong.net/index.htm
[239] http://www.zyq.ca/

Meditation and Contemplation

Meditation refers to a practice whereby the practitioner (meaning the individual in question) can train their minds and/or self-induce a specific mode of consciousness in order to realize some personally derived benefit.

Meditation, then, is generally an inwardly oriented, personal practice of mental discipline.

Meditation is a practice whereby you learn how to still the mind "so that it will do what you want it to do, rather than what it has already been programmed to do. In Meditation, you learn to ignore the flow of ideas, sounds and thoughts, while you are busy, merely being there, [focusing] your consciousness upon your consciousness, rather than upon the objects of your consciousness [because in] this stillness lies the power to overcome and to create." [240]

---

[240] Lewis, James Clair. *Contemplation and Meditation* article accessed on November 12, 2011 at
http://www.jamesclairlewis.com/pages/metaphysics/meditation.html

Contemplation is a process whereby "one takes an object or principle and focuses upon it. Your concentration becomes immersed in the object of contemplation, until you become one with it. Images, trains of ideas and thoughts concerning [that which] you are contemplating, come to your mind, revealing [their] true nature. Contemplation is a great tool for discovering truth. Mathematicians and theoretical physicists regularly employ contemplation in their researches with great success." [241]

In the West, contemplation basically refers to a content-free mind directed towards the awareness of God as a living reality, which, corresponds, in some ways, to that which is termed Samadhi in the East. [242]

It was Isaac the Syrian who explained the purpose of silence as *awakening the mind to God*. [243]

---

[241] Lewis, James Clair. *Contemplation and Meditation* article accessed on November 12, 2011 at
http://www.jamesclairlewis.com/pages/metaphysics/meditation.html
[242] http://en.wikipedia.org/wiki/Contemplation
[243] http://www.theosophical.org/publications/quest-magazine/1432

Samadhi, then, has been described as "a non-dualistic state of consciousness in which the consciousness of the experiencing subject becomes one with the experienced object, and in which the mind becomes still, one-pointed or concentrated, while the person remains conscious. In Buddhism, it can also refer to an abiding in which mind becomes very still, but does not merge with the object of attention, and is thus able to observe and gain insight into the changing flow of experience." [244]

Sri Nisargadatta Maharaj, a spiritual teacher and philosopher of Advaita (Nondualism) from India describes Samadhi in the following manner.

When "you say you sit for meditation, the first thing to be done is understand that it is not this body identification that is sitting for meditation, but this knowledge 'I am', this consciousness, which is sitting in meditation and is meditating on itself. When this is finally understood, then it becomes easy. When this consciousness, this conscious presence, merges in itself, the state of 'Samadhi' ensues. It

---

[244] http://en.wikipedia.org/wiki/Samadhi

is the conceptual feeling that I exist that disappears and merges into the beingness itself. So this conscious presence also gets merged into that knowledge, that beingness – that is 'Samadhi'." [245]

In accordance with the Eightfold Path (created by Buddha), Samadhi, or concentration of the mind, is the 3rd division that involves right effort, right mindfulness and right meditation. [246]

While the bliss of Samadhi is not the goal of Buddhism, it continues to remain an important tool in reaching the goal of enlightenment.

All of this brings to mind another term of importance, that of introspection, which can be defined as "a conscious and purposive process relying on thinking, reasoning, and examining one's own thoughts, feelings, and, in more spiritual cases, one's soul." [247]

---

[245] http://en.wikipedia.org/wiki/Samadhi
[246] http://en.wikipedia.org/wiki/Eightfold_Path
[247] http://en.wikipedia.org/wiki/Introspection

In the words of William Godwin ... *The philosophy of the wisest man that ever existed, is mainly derived from the act of introspection.*

Introspection (also known as metacognition) involves taking the time to observe one's self, courtesy of the inner workings of their own brain (in relation to their mental processes, thinking and emotional states), which then becomes both one's conscious awareness (of self) as well as one's subjective self-awareness.

Thomas Mann shares that *introspection is the first step towards transformation ... after knowing himself, nobody can continue being the same ...* making it a risky venture for the simple reason that you will find yourself being transformed, no longer able to hold onto the comfort zone of your previous existence.

In the words of Josef Pieper, author of <u>Happiness and Contemplation</u> ... *the greatest menace to our capacity for contemplation is the incessant fabrication of tawdry, empty, stimuli which kill the receptivity of the soul.*

Introspection involves becoming more mindful, wherein careful evaluation, of any given situation, results in a more conscious choice. This is where you find yourself "getting out of the box of personality and consciously shaping your reaction to life events." [248]

One can engage in the process of introspection through reflective journal writing; a way to explore "what we can become without being judged. What we bring to an experience is essential to our understanding of what occurs. This is influenced by our past, our future, and our present world-views; a deeper understanding [is what] enables us to integrate former learning with experiences, to form relationships between parts of knowledge, and to search for meaning. The more we share our thoughts and feelings, the more we challenge accepted views of traditions and myths, which have kept alternate interpretations from becoming possibilities." [249]

---

[248] http://www.lessons4living.com/introspection.htm

[249] http://www.snjourney.com/ClinicalInfo/WrAndReport/ReflectiveWr.htm

What I like about reflective journal writing entries is that they are reflections, snapshots in time, if you will, that often evoke more questions than answers, thereby demonstrating the soul searching that goes hand-in-hand with introspection.

The purpose of these ever developing questions, then, is to assist one in their succinct focusing on the personal meaning (which also equates to one's personal interpretation) associated with that particular reflective moment.

Let's face it; change is the only constant that exists.

Reflective journal writing, then, is but one strategy that can allow an individual to examine the meaning of this change.

According to Nil Celen, introspection is "the key to consciousness, consciousness is the key to the right decision, and the right decision is the key to success." [250]

Advanced Contemplation [251]

---

[250] http://mindpower-scientificproofs.com/introspection-for-conscious-decisions/
[251] http://www.paulbrunton.org/notebooks/23

Contemplation [252]

Contemplation [253]

Contemplative Practices [254]

Higher-Order Theories of Consciousness [255]

Integrating and Converging Four Complementary Practices [256]

Introspective Insights [257]

How to Write a Reflective Journal [258]

Meditation [259]

252

http://www.srichinmoy.org/spirituality/concentration_meditation_cont emplation/contemplation/index.html
[253] http://www.spiritual-endeavors.org/basic/contem.htm
[254] http://www.contemplativemind.org/practices/
[255] http://www.iep.utm.edu/consc-hi/
[256] http://swamij.com/complementary.htm
[257] http://www.dailyom.com/articles/2/2011/30353.html
[258] http://www.ehow.com/how_4610609_write-reflective-journal.html
259

http://www.srichinmoy.org/spirituality/concentration_meditation_cont emplation/meditation/index.html

Meditation: Fanning the Fire [260]

Meditation versus Contemplation [261]

Samadhi [262]

Specific Brain Region Linked to Introspective Thoughts [263]

The Art of Living Consciously: The Power of Awareness to Transform Everyday Life [264]

The Biology of Introspection [265]

The Hole in the Sidewalk [266]

---

[260] http://www.qi-journal.com/Qigong.asp?Name=Meditation: Fanning the Fire&-token.D=Article

[261] http://www.srichinmoy.org/spirituality/concentration_meditation_cont emplation/contemplation/meditation_vs_contemplation/index.html

[262] http://www.srichinmoy.org/spirituality/concentration_meditation_cont emplation/samadhi/index.html

[263] http://www.aaas.org/news/releases/2010/0916sp_introspection.shtml?s a_campaign=Internal_Ads/AAAS/AAAS_News/2010-09-16/jump_page

[264] http://www.amazon.com/dp/0684838494/

[265] http://www.science20.com/news_articles/biology_introspection

[266] http://www.lessons4living.com/sidewalk_of_life.htm

The Pitfalls of Meditation: Dazed by Sensation [267]

The Power of Introspection [268]

The Self: Understanding What and Who We Are [269]

Transformation and Transcendence [270]

Why Meditation is Important in Martial Arts [271]

[267] http://www.qi-journal.com/Qigong.asp?-token.D=Article&-MaxRecords=1&-SkipRecords=0&-Op=bw&Name=The%20Pitfalls%20of%20Meditation%3a%20Dazed%20by%20Sensation
[268] http://comfortfoodforthesoul.com/the-power-of-introspection-looking-inside-to-get-back-on-track/
[269] http://knol.google.com/k/the-self#
[270] http://www.angelfire.com/hi/TheSeer/transcend.html
[271] http://www.qi-journal.com/Qigong.asp?Name=Why Meditation Is Important in Martial Arts&-token.D=Article

Mindfulness

Mindfulness is what constitutes my mind training. While mind training is required if one is to become a Jedi Knight, mindfulness is my own choice.

To transcend the mind is comparable to watching your thoughts and feelings pass by, choosing which thought and/or feeling to entertain at any given moment.

While stilling the chatter of the mind can aid in mental and physical relaxation, what is even more important is recognizing and acknowledging that you are not your mind.

Transcending the dualistic mind is the battle of surrendering the bullying of the mind (ego-dominated existence) to mindfulness (awareness of one's thoughts, actions and motivations).

Mindfulness means being aware of the moment in which we are living.

Mindfulness is meditation in action, allowing life to unfold without the limitation of prejudgment.

Mindfulness means being open to awareness whilst also becoming the Infinite Possibilitarian that author Norman Vincent Peale addresses in his work.

Mindfulness pertains to existing in a relaxed state of attentiveness, one that involves both the inner world of thoughts and feelings, as well as the outer world of actions and perceptions.

Choosing at least one activity each day, to carry out in a mindful manner (giving it your full attention), helps considerably.

If you are chopping vegetables, take the time to absorb the colors, the textures, the smells, the motions, the tastes.

If you are exercising on a treadmill, take the time to feel your muscles moving as you walk, run, jog, speed up, slow down.

That having been said, one can learn to live the entirety of their day in mindful meditation.

There is no witness. There is no judgment. You have succeeded in becoming an observer without engaging the mind.

Thoughts and feelings are simply thoughts and feelings. They are not who you are.

Before one can work toward transcending the mind, one must reprogram (reconfigure) the subconscious mind.

This is what I had to do in order to eclipse a life filled with total negative media bombardment.

Meditation is but one avenue open to the seeker.

At first, you will hear your own thoughts forming in your mind. You may quickly come to realize that there tends to be much continuous repetition to your thoughts.

Herein lies the greatest challenge, for there will be many thoughts that will arise as you are attempting to meditate.

In the very beginning, you will find yourself getting lost in them. Trying to remain unattached, to the chatter in your head, is the most difficult part.

You merely wish to become an observer, standing at the sidelines, if you will. As soon as you pass judgment on what you are observing, the thoughts will drag you down.

Pretend that you are outside, observing the clouds as they float across the sky. Now imagine your thought forms as the very clouds that are passing you by.

It is in coming to this realization that you can honestly say *I have become a witness to my own mind.*

There may also be pictures and images that begin to filter through. Try to become a witness to these as well.

Do not engage with either the thoughts or the images. Simply accept them while remaining unattached. Do not judge them. Remember, you are merely the observer.

You may also notice your body responding (emotional reactions) to specific thought forms that are filtering through. Once again, you must step out of the emotion.

One should not allow an emotion to control them while in the physical body. You are merely the observer. You may continue to be the witness, but only without judgment.

Even though *becoming a witness* to thought forms, pictures, images and emotions, is not an easy task, it is something that *needs to be practiced every day*.

As you are able to experience success with this while in a meditative state, so, too, shall you be able to practice *living a waking meditation* throughout your entire day.

While it is imperative that you become aware of what goes on in your mind, when you are going about your daily life, it is important that you continue to step back, thereby maintaining the stance of an objective observer.

When you are able to experience this with considerable success, you can say that you are practicing a mindfulness type of meditation.

It is also important to realize that there is a monumental difference between you (as the observer) and the things that are observed by you.

As you become more of a witness to your own mind, your consciousness is becoming more aware of itself.

What this means is that the egoic mind will begin to become quiet so that you can learn to reside, in a pure and nonjudgmental way, in what can be called the *real* Self.

All of the varied forms of meditation have but one purpose: to introduce you to the experiencing of consciousness. With this, then, comes the realization that this is all there is.

As you dedicate yourself to this practice, on an intense and daily basis, you will begin to observe transformation on many levels, each as unique as the being that you are.

In addition to meditation, affirmations and visualizations can also be used as transformational tools, a way of bypassing the conscious mind.

Affirmations are personal statements written in both positive and present tense terms. The more emotion one evokes upon saying these affirmations aloud, the more powerful they become.

When it comes to visualization, yet another medium, I find it incredibly difficult to see the pictures while also trying to put myself in the image. It is quite difficult to get emotionally excited about a specific impression, when all my mind sees are some dark and fuzzy attempts at a new reality.

Now that I have discovered Mind Movies,[272] an absolutely phenomenal metaphysical tool, I am able to visualize with increasing clarity.

Freedom experienced on an inner level is the very freedom that all seek, for it *is the real freedom*. This is what you experience when you are able to still the mind.

A calm mind is a powerful mind.

---

[272] http://www.mindmovies.com/?10107

Peace, contentment, happiness and bliss are to be found when one experiences this silence, this stillness, this sense of calm.

Accordingly, there are also additional benefits.

You will find that your ability to concentrate improves.

You will find that you have more patience, showing more tact in responding to difficult situations.

You will find that others do not hold as much sway over you (what they think of you and say about you) as before.

You will find yourself responding to situations with less anxiety and worry.

As difficulties arise, you will demonstrate an increased ability to maintain a sense of inner poise and common sense.

You will find that you are sleeping better.

In addition, all of the above vastly improves your ability to meditate.

Inner peace enables one to feel grounded, to feel balanced. In these stressful times, this is what is needed by all.

Developing the ability to still the mind will take you a considerable distance towards attaining, and maintaining, inner balance and peace of mind.

Mindfulness [273]

Mindfulness [274]

Mindfulness [275]

Mindfulness [276]

Mindfulness and Kindness: Inner Sources of Freedom and Happiness [277]

Mindfulness-Based Stress Reduction (MBSR) [278]

---

[273] http://dharma.ncf.ca/introduction/instructions/sati.html
[274] http://www.psychologytoday.com/basics/mindfulness
[275] http://www.get.gg/mindfulness.htm
[276] http://www.springer.com/psychology/journal/12671
[277] http://www.jimhopper.com/mindfulness/
[278] http://www.meditationforhealth.com/

Mindfulness Meditation Centre [279]

Mindfulness Practice Community of Vancouver [280]

Mindfulness Retreats [281]

The Mindfulness Bell Magazine [282]

The Mindfulness Guide for the Super Busy: How to Live Life to the Fullest [283]

The Mindfulness Institute [284]

---

[279] http://www.mindfulnessmeditationcentre.org/
[280] http://mindfulnessvancouver.org/
[281] http://www.tnhtour.org/
[282] http://iamhome.org/thay.php
[283] http://zenhabits.net/the-mindfulness-guide-for-the-super-busy-how-to-live-life-to-the-fullest/
[284] http://www.mindfulnessinstitute.ca/Home.aspx

Intuitiveness

Intuitiveness, something we all possess, is equated with intuition; generally speaking, it can be described as the power to discern (detect, know, perceive, recognize) the true nature of a person or situation (using such words as insight, instinct, sixth sense).

The ability to notice "the subtle signals of intuition requires mindfulness of the self. Intuition can come in many forms, and being mindful of thoughts, physical sensations, and emotional reactions, is an important part of recognizing and attending to those subtle signals." [285]

How do I attune with my intuition? I simply take the time to stop, breathe and listen to my heart.

Developing Intuition [286]

---

[285] *Easy Ways to Develop Intuition with Meditation* article accessed on November 12, 2011 at http://c-ann-logsdon.suite101.com/easy-ways-to-develop-intuition-with-meditation-a119945
[286] http://www.theharbinger.org/xvii/981201/robinson.html

Developing Intuition [287]

Developing Intuition [288]

Developing Intuition [289]

Five Steps to Intuitive Healing [290]

Holistic Intuition Society [291]

How to Develop Your Intuition [292]

Institute of Noetic Sciences [293]

Intuition [294]

Intuitive Development [295]

---

[287] http://www.creativelivinginc.com/intuition.htm
[288] http://www.vibrani.com/intuition.htm
[289] http://www.effective-mind-control.com/developing-intuition.html
[290] http://www.drjudithorloff.com/Free-Articles/Five-Steps.htm
[291] http://www.in2it.ca/
[292] http://www.essentiallifeskills.net/develop-your-intuition.html
[293] http://www.noetic.org/topics/intuition/
[294] http://www.davidstyles.com/intuition/
[295] http://www.withinsight.com/intuition/#

Shakti Gawain, Developing Intuition, Part 1 [296]

Shakti Gawain, Developing Intuition, Part 2 [297]

Shakti Gawain, Developing Intuition, Part 3 [298]

Shakti Gawain, Developing Intuition, Part 4 [299]

Silva Intuition System [300]

The School of Insight and Intuition [301]

The Science of Innate Intelligence [302]

Trusting Our Internal Guide [303]

What Is Intuition [304]

---

[296] http://www.spiritsite.com/writing/shagaw/part14.shtml
[297] http://www.spiritsite.com/writing/shagaw/part15.shtml
[298] http://www.spiritsite.com/writing/shagaw/part16.shtml
[299] http://www.spiritsite.com/writing/shagaw/part17.shtml
[300] http://www.silvaintuitionsystem.com/
[301] http://www.insightandintuition.com/
[302] http://www.angelfire.com/hi/TheSeer/Lipton.html
[303] http://www.creating-positive-change.com/developing-intuition.html
[304] http://www.eliselebeau.com/intuition

Transcending the Dark Side

Transcending the Dark Side can also be seen as transcending duality, a term that "represents many definitions, including the very nature of our own composite structure, not to mention the entire universe," [305] especially in referencing the terms *light* and *dark*.

In referencing *light*, we speak of attributes such as peace, love, hope, kindness, joy, integrity, fulfillment, sense of purpose, excitement, well-being, compassion, nonjudgment and empathy. So, too, are these the very attributes that can be expressed by all, or not, should that be their choice. The *dark*, by contrast, is generally reserved for such attributes as conflict, fear, despair, judgment, anger, deceit, hatred, bigotry, prejudice; where *the ugly side of our reality* is founded." [306]

---

[305] *The Love of Your Life: Transcending Duality* article accessed on November 12, 2011 at http://spiritlibrary.com/heartlight/the-love-of-your-life-transcending-duality
[306] Ibid.

How, then, do we reconcile "the duality of the light and dark that is at the core of this reality, so we can actually transcend our consciousness beyond the limitations that confront us daily through these two contrasts?" [307]

According to Rumi ... *No opposite can be known without its opposite. If duality did not exist, how would we know enough to yearn and strive for wholeness, for completion, for unity?* There is much truth to these very words.

There exists a duality in this wondrous Cosmos of ours, an inevitable existence of interconnected opposites: male and female, Yin and Yang, good and evil, day and night, life and death, happiness and sadness, new and old, spirit and body, same and different. Such is the natural law that appears to govern the whole of creation and life as we know it, and yet there are proponents who claim that duality means believing that we are alone, that we are isolated from others, that we are separate from All That Is.

---

[307] *The Love of Your Life: Transcending Duality* article accessed on November 12, 2011 at http://spiritlibrary.com/heartlight/the-love-of-your-life-transcending-duality

Living the Jedi Way

It is my belief that all is connected, that all is one. In remembering our divine nature, we are both the whole and the parts of the whole; the interconnected totality of all life. Such is where duality begins to blur, changing to nonduality.

This is where we begin to comprehend that we must strive to find the oneness, the unconditional love, the peace of mind, that exists beyond the duality of our experience.

Nonduality lets us see that all is connected, that all is unified. In realizing that we share a oneness, we come to terms with the fact that we are no longer separate.

All that exists is the here and now; hence, we are neither winner, nor loser; we are neither victim, nor perpetrator.

There is no right or wrong, for the Creator has allowed both *light* and *dark* to exist so that we may come to know ourselves in all ways.

To transcend duality, we need to know that "everything just *is* and every human being is where they need to be, experiencing what is necessary for their highest good." [308] It is our job, however, to "find the lesson within the experience which, then, becomes a gift to ourselves." [309]

As stated before, there is a purpose to duality. We are here to experience both the *light* and the *dark* so that we may "emerge from the illusion knowing everything is as it should be and is always for our highest good. For those still caught in the illusion, this concept is usually not received well, but until we choose to expand our awareness and truly embrace the journey completely, we remain trapped in judgment and blame." [310]

There is nothing in the universe that is separate from the Creator, meaning that even the *dark* side is not separate from the *light*. When "we bring light to any darkness, it dissolves like a lantern in a cave. The darkness is still there, for as soon as the lantern is extinguished it appears just as easily as

---

[308] *The Love of Your Life: Transcending Duality* article accessed on November 12, 2011 at http://spiritlibrary.com/heartlight/the-love-of-your-life-transcending-duality
[309] Ibid.
[310] Ibid.

it dissolved. If one happened to be lost in a cave, the situation does not change by lighting the lantern, however, it allows one to see the situation with a clearer vision to find the way out. In this scenario we are neither the light nor the dark, but the observer who has transcended the duality of the experience." [311]

In retrospect, we are here to wake up to who we really are through the experience of duality.

When we, as a collective, can "also live from this place and look down on the duality in our own lives and shine our light on the dark side, it is in that moment [that] we [will] have transcended into a higher level of consciousness. This act of unconditional love [is what] ultimately frees the world from this perceived illusion, but it has to start with our own lives." [312]

---

[311] *The Love of Your Life: Transcending Duality* article accessed on November 12, 2011 at http://spiritlibrary.com/heartlight/the-love-of-your-life-transcending-duality
[312] Ibid.

In our ability "to ignite the lantern to disperse the darkness, with the knowledge that everything is in order, no matter where we find ourselves," [313] this is the path to freedom; the path that each must find.

Collective consciousness is the greatest power we have as human beings, meaning that "each is connected to the other, making up the ocean of humanity. As the waves rise and return to the ocean, we realize that we have never been separate from each other. Rather, [it is] the duality of the land and the sea, the expanse of the sky and depths of the ocean, [that] are but a different experience of the one creation. When we [are able to] see through the eyes of the creator, a knowing arises that nothing is neither good nor bad, but just is." [314]

Transcending the ego (which can also be referenced as the Dark Side) involves "changing your identity from believing that you are your mind, emotions, habits, attachments, and

---

[313] *The Love of Your Life: Transcending Duality* article accessed on November 12, 2011 at http://spiritlibrary.com/heartlight/the-love-of-your-life-transcending-duality
[314] Ibid.

desires to a larger perspective, where you know you are your Divine Self. You let go of thinking you are a small, isolated, suffering self and open to the magnificence and grandeur of who you truly are (your Divine Self)." [315]

It is in the coming together of all duality (male and female, Yin and Yang, day and night, life and death, happiness and sadness, old and new, body and spirit, same and different), and the embracement and acceptance of the dual parts of the self (*light* and *dark*), that nonduality becomes the reality.

Ultimately, it is this that shall lead to the healing of all, including the patriarchal institutions of old.

When the two become as one, therein shall you find the true Holy Grail.

What does this mean? Is it deliberately meant to be cryptic in nature? Is it meant only for those who have eyes to see and ears to hear?

---

[315] http://www.orindaben.com/catalog/prodno/DS101/

Every individual is on a journey of self; a journey of rediscovery, if you will.

In the integration of the dualistic parts of the self (light and dark, love and hate, masculine and feminine), we are able to revert back to our truest nature: one of compassion and compassionate allowing; thereby leading to the reestablishment of one's creative powers through the balancing of the self.

It shall be in this rediscovering of our true selves that we will have found the Holy Grail.

While the Holy Grail is the same for everyone, the process and experience(s) for each individual shall be vastly different; hence, we all become the Grail.

In having identified that there is something great at work, every time you are at peace, so, too, are you enlightened.

Inner peace is probably the most important thing that can be attained.

When you experience inner peace, you are truly happy and content with your Self. Your state of mind is a quiet mind and you are completely connected to God(dess).

God(dess) and peace are synonymous. Inner turmoil is what suffocates your spirit, thereby preventing you from living from your higher self, unable to see life with a greater sense of clarity.

Enlightenment (the Holy Grail) is a state of being whereby you are reunited with your true spiritual self. It is this connectedness, this freedom of the self, that leads us to the ultimate and definitive realization that we are all one, thus imbuing our bodies with a sense of inner peace that allows us to joyfully accept and live life as per our creation.

We must take the time to revisit the message that Yeshua ben Yosef (Jesus) attempted to share with us 2,000 years ago, as opposed to that which has been corrupted, hijacked, fabricated and manufactured in his name, for therein lies the necessary truth(s).

Seek ye knowledge and ye shall find the truth that liberates. Seek ye discipline in the persisting with positive thoughts. Seek ye the joy of creating, the joy of learning, the joy of experiencing. Seek ye the realm of infinite possibilities for therein ye shall find the all. Seek ye the seer that ye be. [316]

As Osho has written ......

Consciousness can do two things: it can create ego, it can create egolessness. If it creates ego, you live in hell, if it creates egolessness, you are in paradise. The whole world is in paradise without knowing it. When man enters paradise he will be entering with full knowing. That is the grandeur, the beauty of man — and that is the danger also, because out of thousands of people, only once in a while does a person enter; others simply go on falling into the trap of the ego. Be egoless and all the grace of God is yours. Bliss is by the grace of God. [317]

---

[316] Doucette, Michele. (2010) *Veracity At Its Best* (page 141). McMinnville, TN: St. Clair Publications.
[317] http://www.oshoquotes.net/2011/06/osho-on-bliss-be-egoless-and-all-the-grace-of-god-is-yours/

Escaping Tatooine and the Cause of Suffering [318]

Jerry Katz on Nonduality [319]

Let Go The Ego [320]

Nonduality Satsang: Nova Scotia [321]

Nonduality: The Varieties of Expression (Jerry Katz) [322]

Osho: Insights on Ego [323]

Osho: Quotes on Ego [324]

---

[318] http://lorimgrant.com/2009/05/25/escaping-tatooine-the-cause-of-suffering/
[319] http://nonduality.org/
[320]
http://www.lifepositive.com/Mind/Personal_Growth/Let_go_the_ego7 2005.asp
[321] http://nonduality.ca/
[322] http://www.nonduality.com/
[323] http://www.oshoquotes.net/2011/06/osho-when-you-are-absolutely-pure-the-ego-disappears/
[324] http://www.oshoquotes.net/2010/08/osho-quotes-on-ego-osho-sayings-on-ego/

Self-Awareness and Humility: Lessons Not Learned by
Anakin [325]

Science and Nonduality (SAND) [326]

The Dark Side: Beyond Good and Evil [327]

The Dharma of Star Wars: Learning about the Dark Side
Within [328]

The Eightfold Path: Transcending the Dark Side [329]

Transcend Duality and Rise Above Dichotomies [330]

---

[325] http://lorimgrant.com/2009/05/23/self-awareness-and-humility-
lessons-not-learned-by-anakin/
[326] http://www.scienceandnonduality.com/nonduality.shtml
[327]
http://www.christiananswersforthenewage.org/Articles_DarkSide1.ht
ml
[328] http://lorimgrant.com/2009/05/24/the-dharma-of-star-wars-
learning-about-the-dark-side-within/
[329] http://lorimgrant.com/2009/05/26/the-eightfold-path-transcending-
the-dark-side/
[330] http://ginigrey.com/spiritualtransformers/transcend-duality-and-
rise-above-dichotomies/

Transcending and Including the Ego [331]

Transcending Dualistic Thinking [332]

Transcending Duality (Alan Watts MP3 audio) [333]

Transcending Duality [334]

Transcending Ego: Distinguishing Consciousness from Wisdom [335]

Transcending the Ego [336]

Transcending the Ego [337]

Transcending the Illusion of Duality [338]

---

[331] http://www.illuminatedmind.net/2008/04/01/transcending-and-including-the-ego/
[332] http://www.alcoholanddrugabuse.com/article_dualistic_thinking.html
[333] http://www.illuminatiarchives.org/occult/alan-watts-audio-mp3-downloads/
[334] http://www.godlikeproductions.com/forum1/message655800/pg1
[335] http://www.rinpoche.com/teachings/conwisdom.pdf
[336] http://ezinearticles.com/?Spiritual-Life-Coaching:-Transcending-the-Ego&id=6354198
[337] http://independentspirituality.com/transcending-the-ego/
[338] http://www.2012spiritual.info/oneness--transcending-duality.html

What Is Advaita or Nonduality? [339]

What Is Ego: Friend or Foe? [340]

What Is It About Star Wars? [341]

Wisdom and Compassion: Luke Transcends Suffering [342]

Witnessing the Mind [343]

Could it not be said that, on a comparable note, transcending the Dark Side might also be referenced as having escaped the Matrix?

---

[339] http://endless-satsang.com/advaita-nonduality-oneness.htm
[340] http://www.enlightennext.org/magazine/j17/j17.asp
[341] http://lorimgrant.com/2009/05/22/what-is-it-about-star-wars/
[342] http://lorimgrant.com/2009/05/27/wisdom-and-compassion-luke-transcends-suffering/
[343] http://www.yoga-mind-control.com/witnessing-the-mind.html

Ma'at

Ma'at, the Ancient Egyptian concept of truth, justice, balance (harmony), order and moral law, was personified as a goddess regulating the stars, seasons, and the actions of both mortals and the deities, who set the order of the universe from chaos at the moment of creation. [344]

The earliest surviving records indicating Ma'at as having been the norm, for nature and society, were recorded during the Old Kingdom, with the earliest substantial surviving examples being found in the pyramid texts of Unas (circa 2375 BCE and 2345 BCE). [345]

The symbol associated with Ma'at was the ostrich feather, her emblem, which represented truth.

Thought to be the wife of Thoth, the god of wisdom, she was considered the most important deity of them all.

---

[344] http://en.wikipedia.org/wiki/Maat
[345] Ibid.

Just as it was the duty of the Pharaoh to uphold Ma'at, so, too, is it your duty to uphold the same in your current life.

http://www.rainbowcrystal.com/atext/egypt10.html

Truth and Honesty

In words that have been attributed to Galileo ... *All truths are easy to understand once they are discovered; the point is to discover them.*

John Gilmore said ... *Truth: the most deadly weapon ever discovered by humanity, capable of destroying entire perceptual sets, cultures and realities. Outlawed by all governments everywhere, possession is normally punishable by death.*

It was Albert Einstein who wrote ... *The search for truth implies a duty. One must not conceal any part of what one has recognized to be true.*

Chuck Swindoll shared ... *Honesty has a beautiful and refreshing simplicity about it. No ulterior motives; no hidden meanings; an absence of hypocrisy, duplicity, political games, and verbal superficiality. As honesty and real integrity characterize our lives, there will be no need to manipulate others.*

In words that have been attributed to René Descartes ... *In the matter of a difficult question, it is more likely that the truth should have been discovered by the few, than by the many.*

Abraham Lincoln said ... *I am a firm believer in the people. If given the truth, they can be depended upon to meet any national crisis. The great point is to bring them the real facts.*

It was Mahatma Ghandi who wrote ... *Truth resides in every human heart, and one has to search for it there, and to be guided by truth as one sees it. But no one has a right to coerce others to act according to his own view of truth.*

Herbert Sebastien Agar shared ... *The truth that makes men free is, for the most part, the truth which men prefer not to hear.*

In words that have been attributed to Plato ... *False words are not only evil in themselves, but they infect the soul with evil.*

Benjamin Franklin said ... *Half a truth is often a great lie.*

It was Søren Kierkegaard, the Danish philosopher, theologian and chief founder of existentialist thought, who wrote ... *Truth always rests with the minority, and the minority is always stronger than the majority, because the minority is generally formed by those who really have an opinion, while the strength of a majority is illusory, formed by the gangs who have no opinion, and who, therefore, in the next instant (when it is evident that the minority is the stronger) assume its opinion ... while Truth again reverts to a new minority.*

Sir Walter Scott shared .... *Oh, what a wicked web we weave, when first we practice to deceive.*

In words that have been attributed to Shapley R. Hunter ... *The continued utterance of a lie does not make it true, but it does convince many that it is, particularly if you can squelch most efforts to expose the lie.*

George Orwell said ... *In times of universal deceit, telling the truth will be a revolutionary act.*

It was Eugene V. Debs who wrote ... *Do not worry over the charge of treason to your masters, but be concerned about the treason that involves yourselves. Be true to yourself and you cannot be a traitor to any good cause on Earth.*

In words that have been attributed to Gustave LeBon in The Crowd ... *The masses have never thirsted after truth. Whoever can supply them with illusions is easily their master; whoever attempts to destroy their illusions is always their victim.*

Hindu Prince Gautama Siddharta (also known as Buddha) said ... *Believe nothing just because a so-called wise person said it. Believe nothing just because a belief is generally held. Believe nothing just because it is said in ancient books. Believe nothing just because it is said to be of divine origin. Believe nothing just because someone else believes it. Believe only what you, yourself, test and judge to be true.*

It was Alexander Solzhenitsyn, Russian writer, Soviet dissident, imprisoned for 8 years for criticizing Stalin in a personal letter, and Nobel Prize for Literature winner in 1970, who wrote … *The simple step of a courageous individual is not to take part in the lie. One word of truth outweighs the world.*

Johann Wolfgang von Goethe shared … *Wisdom is found only in truth.*

Truth has been a topic of discussion for thousands of years. While the question, *what is truth*, is a very simple one, answering it is not.

In order to best ascertain what truth is, perhaps we need to look further at determining what it is not, meaning that "truth is not error; truth is not self-contradictory; truth is not deception. Of course, it could be true that someone is being deceptive, but the deception itself isn't truth." [346]

---

[346] *What is Truth* article accessed on November 16, 2011 at http://carm.org/secular-movements/relativism/what-truth

Truth does not equate to either the correct concept (as in scientific inquiry) or a set of laws or governing principles (as determined by societal values). Instead, truth is what corresponds to both physical reality and metaphysics.

It was Gottfried Wilhelm Leibniz, a Germain philosopher and mathematician, who, in 1670, wrote ... *Reality cannot be found except in One single source, because of the interconnection of all things with one another.*

It was Jiddu Krishnamurti who stated ... *Truth must be discovered, but there is no formula for its discovery. You must set out on the uncharted sea, and the uncharted sea is yourself. You must set out to discover yourself.*

It was also Jiddu Krishnamurti who wrote ... *No person from outside can make you free. No one holds the Key to the Kingdom of Happiness. No one has the authority to hold that key. That key is your own self, and in the development and the purification and in the incorruptibility of that self alone is the Kingdom of Eternity.*

Can Metaphysics Discover Surprises? (John Searle) [347]

Can Metaphysics Discover Surprises? (Dean Zimmerman) [348]

Can Metaphysics Discover Surprises (Colin McGinn) [349]

Can Metaphysics Discover Surprises? (Hubert Dreyfus) [350]

How Does Metaphysics Reveal Reality? (Hubert Dreyfus) [351]

How Does Metaphysics Reveal Reality? (George Lakoff) [352]

---

[347] http://www.closertotruth.com/video-profile/Can-Metaphysics-Discover-Surprises-John-Searle-/1511
[348] http://www.closertotruth.com/video-profile/Can-Metaphysics-Discover-Surprises-Dean-Zimmerman-/1361
[349] http://www.closertotruth.com/video-profile/Can-Metaphysics-Discover-Surprises-Colin-McGinn-/791
[350] http://www.closertotruth.com/video-profile/Can-Metaphysics-Discover-Surprises-Hubert-Dreyfus-/1520
[351] http://www.closertotruth.com/video-profile/How-Does-Metaphysics-Reveal-Reality-Hubert-Dreyfus-/1518
[352] http://www.closertotruth.com/video-profile/How-Does-Metaphysics-Reveal-Reality-George-Lakoff-/1524

How Does Metaphysics Reveal Reality? (Bas van Fraassen) [353]

How Does Metaphysics Reveal Reality? (Philip Clayton) [354]

How Does Metaphysics Reveal Reality? (Part 1 of 2) (Peter van Inwagen) [355]

How Does Metaphysics Reveal Reality? (Part 2 of 2) (Peter van Inwagen) [356]

On Truth and Reality: The Wave Structure of Matter [357]

Stanford Encyclopedia of Philosophy [358]

---

[353] http://www.closertotruth.com/video-profile/How-does-Metaphysics-Reveal-Reality-Bas-van-Fraassen-/1375
[354] http://www.closertotruth.com/video-profile/How-does-Metaphysics-Reveal-Reality-Philip-Clayton-/1196
[355] http://www.closertotruth.com/video-profile/How-does-Metaphysics-Reveal-Reality-Part-1-of-2-Peter-van-Inwagen-/1086
[356] http://www.closertotruth.com/video-profile/How-does-Metaphysics-Reveal-Reality-Part-2-of-2-Peter-van-Inwagen-/1085
[357] http://www.spaceandmotion.com/
[358] http://plato.stanford.edu/entries/truth/

Integrity

It was Baltasar Gracian, a Spanish philosopher and writer (1601-1658), who wrote ... *A single lie destroys a whole reputation for integrity.*

Integrity is "the quality or condition of being whole, complete, and undivided. The word *integrity* comes from the Latin root word *integer*, which means *a complete entity*."[359]

Integrity is often regarded as the honesty and truthfulness of one's actions; likewise, living a consistent life, in light of the truth, is also referred to as one's integrity.

More importantly, however, integrity refers to "being honest *with yourself* (your wants, needs, feelings, thoughts, hopes, wishes, weaknesses, temptations, dreams, and desires) and

---

[359] *It's Not What You Think It's About* article accessed on November 17, 2011 at http://www.swatinstitute.com/blog/its-not-what-you-think-its-about/

having the courage to share your truth and make the changes you need in order to become a whole, complete entity." [360]

Living a life of integrity is about aligning yourself (your thoughts, words, and actions) with *who you really are*, not who you've been or who you fear becoming." [361]

Individuals with integrity ......

[1] refuse to settle for less than what they know they deserve.

[2] ask for what they want (and need) from others.

[3] speak their truth (even though it might create conflict).

[4] behave in ways that are in alignment (harmony) with who they really are.

[5] make choices based on what they believe (as opposed to what others believe).

---

[360] *It's Not What You Think It's About* article accessed on November 17, 2011 at http://www.swatinstitute.com/blog/its-not-what-you-think-its-about/
[361] Ibid.

[6] value the inner things (that matter most) as opposed to the outer things that are purely temporal.

[7] have a vision for themselves.

Those with integrity *"know who they are, like who they are, and trust themselves in the highest regard."* [362] So, too, do they respect themselves.

If you live a life that it in harmony with your spiritual values, you are living a life of integrity.

If you live a life that espouses basic human dignity, you are living a life of integrity.

If you live a life of sincerity to self, by being true to yourself and who you really are, you are living a life of integrity.

If you have the courage to live your purpose, you are living a life of integrity.

---

[362] *It's Not What You Think It's About* article accessed on November 17, 2011 at http://www.swatinstitute.com/blog/its-not-what-you-think-its-about/

When you are living a life of integrity, you are able to "live a life free of worry and fear." [363]

We all have a part to play when it comes to living with integrity.

In endeavoring to become such a person, you must "let your actions be in conformity with your words ... [by doing] the right thing, even if nobody is watching. In the wise words of Paul Wellstone, *Never separate the life you live from the words you speak.*" [364]

Spencer Johnson said ... *Integrity is telling myself the truth and honesty is telling the truth to other people.*

Truth always allows you to live with integrity.

In essence, you are here to be all that you can be.

Core Value: Integrity [365]

---

[363] *Living with Integrity* article accessed on November 18, 2011 at http://www.motivation-for-dreamers.com/living-with-integrity.html
[364] Ibid.
[365] http://www.egajones.com/2011/09/core-value-integrity/

Living the Jedi Way

Finding My Voice [366]

High Integrity Living [367]

Integrity [368]

Integrity: What It Is and What It Means [369]

Live with Integrity [370]

Living in Integrity [371]

Living in Integrity [372]

Living in Integrity [373]

Living Your Values, Part 1 [374]

---

[366] http://willingnesstogrow.com/tag/living-life-with-integrity/
[367] http://highintegrityliving.com/
[368] http://julialeeyoga.com/post/7553050007/integrity
[369] http://www.drlwilson.com/ARTICLES/INTEGRITY.htm
[370] http://randomthoughtsonlifeblog.com/2011/07/25/live-with-integrity/
[371] http://www.michaelppowers.com/wisdom/integrity.html
[372] http://www.onecommunityranch.org/living-in-integrity/
[373] http://nurturingyoursuccessblog.com/living-in-integrity/
[374] http://www.stevepavlina.com/articles/living-your-values-1.htm

Living Your Values, Part 2 [375]

Living with Integrity [376]

Living with Integrity [377]

New Age: Living with Integrity [378]

Rules to Live By [379]

The Wheel of Integrity [380]

Uphold Your Dignity [381]

What Does Integrity Mean? [382]

---

[375] http://www.stevepavlina.com/articles/living-your-values-2.htm
[376] http://www.lightomega.org/Ind/Pure/Integrity.html
[377] http://www.legalsecretaryjournal.com/?q=living_with_integrity
[378] http://www.marcome.com/blog/new-age-living-with-integrity/
[379] http://howtoloveyourself.me/rules-to-live-by-loving-yourself/
[380] http://powerofbreath.com/articles/the-wheel-of-integrity/
[381] http://www.realmaninc.org/index_files/Page3723.htm
[382] http://www.positive-deviant.com/what-does-integrity-mean.html

Peace and Harmony

Many Buddhists believe that "world peace can only be achieved if we first establish peace within our minds." [383] I, too, am a firm believer in this philosophy.

In keeping, it was Siddhārtha Gautama, the founder of Buddhism, who said *Peace comes from within*; *do not seek it without*; the idea being that anger and other negative states (of mind) are the cause of wars and fighting, meaning that people can live in peace and harmony if they are able to abandon negative emotions, cultivating positive emotions, such as love and compassion, in their stead. [384]

Let's face it, there have been moments whereby many have experienced the true joys of living (in the experiencing of calm, peace, serenity and tranquility), so we know what it looks like, what it tastes like, what it feels like, within our own experience.

---

[383] http://en.wikipedia.org/wiki/World_peace
[384] Ibid.

Connection, caring, cooperation and compassion; these are what constitute harmony.

The Indigenous peoples have long lived in balanced harmony with the totality of creation, taking only what was needed. This is a principle of great importance that we must learn to embrace once again.

Living in harmony with nature (while protecting both the environment as well as other living beings that inhabit the planet), requires that we become stewards (guardians) of Mother Earth.

She, too, is a living organism, that needs to be nurtured, and cared for, in a loving manner.

Living in balanced harmony with nature, and each other, allows one to rediscover the ancient wisdom of love, inner peace and happiness.

Harmony is both an ancient social ideal as well as an actual life choice.

How, then, does one, work to promote harmony?

The foremost necessity becomes *being able to forgive and forget the past*; one must always be prepared to start anew.

Unless you actually "see something for your own selves, or hear it with your own ears, do not believe it. If somebody tells you something unbecoming, know that a man has different moods; we are not perfect. If we have love for others, that very love beautifies even the worst of things. You have to see from that level. That is the only way." [385]

In taking the word world (w-o-r-l-d) and eliminating the letter L from the word, "what remains is Word. The Word is God. If you eliminate yourself (the ego), the thought that you are doing it, you are God's. You become the mouthpiece of God." [386]

These are most profound words, are they not?

---

[385] *Harmony* excerpt from a talk with Sant Kirpal Singh in Washington, DC, on September 2, 1963 accessed on April 23, 2011 at http://www.kirpalsingh-teachings.org/index.php/en/talks/431-harmony.html

[386] Ibid.

In remaining true to your divine selves, in appreciating those around you (for whatever it is that they are able to do), in working for the sake of the common cause (as in the greater good), in living your best each day, know that God(dess) is continuing to work through you.

Mind at Peace

When the mind is at peace,

the world, too, is at peace.

Nothing real, nothing absent.

Not holding on to reality,

not getting stuck in the void,

you are neither holy or wise, just

an ordinary fellow who has completed his work.

P'ang Yün (龐蘊 Hõ Un) (The Enlightened Heart 34) [387]

It becomes in *stilling the mind* (also known as mindfulness) that one attains inner peace; such has been most true for me.

---

[387] http://www.sacred-texts.com/bud/zen/poems.htm

Achieving Peace Through Inner Peace [388]

A Human Approach to World Peace [389]

Attaining Inner Peace and Mental Mastery [390]

Attaining Inner Peace with Meditation [391]

Buddhist Faith and Inner Peace [392]

Feng Shui Tips to Attract Peace and Harmony [393]

Find Inner Peace in 10 Ways [394]

---

[388]
http://www.berzinarchives.com/web/en/archives/approaching_buddhis
m/world_today/achieving_peace_through_inner_peace.html
[389] http://www.dalailama.com/messages/world-peace/a-human-
approach-to-peace
[390]
http://www.successconsciousness.com/innerpeace_mentalmastery.htm
[391] http://www.holisticjunction.com/articles/Attaining-Inner-Peace-
with-Meditation.html
[392] http://buddhistfaith.tripod.com/newmexico/id16.html
[393] http://sachiniti.wordpress.com/2007/01/04/a-few-feng-shui-tips/
[394] http://www.ineedmotivation.com/blog/2008/05/find-inner-peace-in-
10-ways/

Finding Inner Peace and Harmony [395]

Global Peace Initiative [396]

Harmony and Peace Within [397]

How to Find Inner Peace [398]

How to Find Inner Peace: 5 Timeless Thoughts [399]

John Lennon Monument [400]

Learn and Practice Meditation [401]

Living in Peace and Harmony [402]

---

[395] http://advancedlifeskills.com/blog/finding-inner-peace-and-harmony/
[396] http://www.theglobalpeaceinitiative.com/
[397] http://www.disciplelight.com/learning/living/harmony_within
[398] http://www.selfgrowth.com/articles/Sinclair11.html
[399] http://www.positivityblog.com/index.php/2010/02/26/how-to-find-inner-peace-5-timeless-thoughts/
[400] http://www.beatlesstory.com/our-attraction/john-lennon-monument.html
[401] http://www.giftofpeace.org/try2.html
[402]

http://www.chyennemorningstar.com/Peace_Harmony__Respect_Silence.html

Love Peace Harmony Movement [403]

Message of Peace and Harmony Through Arts [404]

Oneness Becomes Us All [405]

Positive Affirmations [406]

Steps Toward Inner Peace [407]

Sustaining Peace and Harmony [408]

The Gift of Inner Peace (movie) [409]

The Gift of Inner Peace (movie download) [410]

World Peace Technology [411]

---

[403] http://www.lovepeaceharmonymovement.com/who-is-master-sha/
[404] http://sites.google.com/site/societyofartists/isa/7-message-of-peace-and-harmony-through-arts
[405] http://onenessbecomesus.com/
[406] http://www.vitalaffirmations.com/affirmations.htm
[407] http://www.peacepilgrim.com/FoPP/htm/steps.htm
[408] http://www.orindaben.com/pages/newsletters/x47_01_peace/
[409] http://www.giftofpeace.org/play_movie.html
[410] http://www.giftofpeace.org/download.html
[411] http://www.worldpeacetech.com/peace%20poems.htm

Understanding

There are exciting, wonderful and beautiful things happening on the planet, many of which are extremely promising.

For example, "on the one hand, we have this carcass of an old world that is dying. It is going through the death throes. And yet, here is this new world that has already been born, and is growing and is going to continue for thousands of years. It isn't going to be the end of *the* world: it is the end of *an old world* and the simultaneous establishment of a *new* one. We are already in the early stages of the golden era of the human race." [412]

It is so true when Dr. Greer shares that "the entirety of creation is sacred and every being is sacred, because spirit, the awake Being, is the very fabric of all that there is. And it is always perfectly one, even if it's playing and displaying

---

[412] Greer, Steven. (2006). *Hidden Truth - Forbidden Knowledge* (p 226). Crozet, VA: Crossing Point, Inc.

upon itself as if it is different. The challenge is to see the oneness within the difference, and also enjoy the difference." [413]

The only constant in life is change. Change allows all to Be (as they are) and to Become (who they truly are).

One of the most challenging tasks we face is to learn to become nonjudgmental.

As you learn to let things be, disentangling from both emotionally charged situations as well as from the collective intellectual mindset of laws, rules and dogma, you are able to experience your own freedom and resolution.

Willing to embrace the higher vibration, an internal shift in consciousness takes place, thereby enabling you to Become (who you truly are).

Do not try to restrict others by judging them, controlling them or blaming them, for this limits your understanding of

---

[413] Greer, Steven. (2006). *Hidden Truth - Forbidden Knowledge* (p 270). Crozet, VA: Crossing Point, Inc.

them. By direct association, this behavior also serves to limit their understanding of themselves.

Just as you have experienced yours, so, too, must you allow others the time and opportunity to experience their own freedom, their own resolution, moving forward as best they know how.

Whenever you judge people or situations, you envelop them within your own belief system. In this way, you blind yourself to the truth about them, forgetting that they, too, are whole and divine.

The way to remembering the sacredness of all life is the way of nonjudgment.

As you become aware of your limiting beliefs, you better understand that your interactions with others are driven by what you believe to be true about the person. Sadly, these limiting beliefs never reflect the actual truth, a truth that states all is one.

As you gain in universal awareness, you quickly come to the realization that your divinity is also theirs as well.

When you respond to people with love and compassion, you readily move from conflict to harmony; such is the very freedom sought by all.

When you remember, embrace and share your divinity, you free others to walk their truth. You become accepting of their truth, for such is whom they are.

So, too, do you remember that we are *continually evolving and changing* as per our own individual experience(s).

This also adds to both the greater collective experience as well as the totality of God, which means that *God is also continually evolving and changing.*

How could it be otherwise for this loving energy that is ongoing and forever?

Long have you been taught to believe that God is perfect, but this is not the case, for perfection is naught but a limitation.

God simply is.

In fact, God loves us so grandly that we have been allowed, through choice and free will, to create our vast illusions of perfection and imperfection, good and evil, positive and negative.

What does this mean?

It means that God, being the totality of All That Is, is the wrong *as well as* the right, the vile ugliness *as well as* the alluring beauty, the unholiness *as well as* the divinity, the illusion *as well as* the reality.

In truth, there is no greater love than this.

We have been entrusted with the power(s) to create that which will enable us to *expand in our knowingness*.

God allows us to express as we choose, without judgment.

We alone determine how, and to what degree, we progress along our evolutionary path, moving past our illusions of limitation to the freedom that lies beyond.

We create the life opportunities of our choice.

We determine and select which path(s) to take. It is to be remembered that the primary tool for this journey is naught but life itself.

Aside from love on an immaculately grand scale, what else holds all matter together?

The answer to this question is thought, for *this*, too, is what God is.

It is known that thought must first exist before manifestation of thought, also known as creation, can take place. In that alignment, we have the ability to manifest whatever we wish, all for the sole purpose of enhancing the wisdom that we continue to accrue, life after life after life.

We create our lives through our own thought processes. Everything you think, you will feel. Everything you feel, you will manifest. Everything you manifest serves to create the condition(s) of your life.

Every word we utter expresses some feeling within our souls. Every word we utter serves to create the conditions of our lives. This is a direct fusion of thought with emotion.

Many will have heard the phrase *like attracts like*, which means that what one gives thought to attracts, unto itself, the very same.

In the end, it is still a matter of choice and free will.

Thought is the true giver of life that never dies, that can never be destroyed. All have used it to think themselves into life, for thought is your link to the mind of God.

We *get* what we speak. We *are* what we think. We *become* what we direct our energies to. We *become* that which we conclude ourselves to be.

That having been said, *I AM THAT I AM* is not a phrase to be taken lightly.

Hence, we are neither slave, nor servant. By comparison, we are sovereign and masterful beings.

We are the creators and directors of our lives.

We write the script and decide who plays the roles assigned to them.

While many continue to accept limiting thoughts, of which there are a significant number (including fear, guilt, despair, unworthiness, failure, worry, unhappiness, pity, misery, hatred, dissension, denial of self), into their lives, it must be remembered that this is neither good nor bad. Coming from a place of nonjudgment, it simply is.

In the end, we must summon into mind that *everything comes down to personal choice.*

Ultimately, you can create a heaven on earth for yourself just as easily as you can create your own hell. Truly the creator of our world(s), we are part of all that we see and all that has ever been.

Here is another profound truth.

While all things are derived from thought, which is God, it is equally important to realize that God is not simply one formulated thought, but the reality of *all* thoughts.

Individual truths, as held by you, as held by me, are *all* true, for each expresses the truth(s) of one's experience at any given moment in time.

199

While there is truth in all things, so, too, is there refinement in all things.

In fact, each moment serves to refine truth, which is why God is *not* a state of perfection, but rather a state of Becoming.

What all are here to inevitably learn is that you, alone, are your greatest teacher. You, alone, are your greatest friend.

Cease looking outside of yourself, for the path you are to follow resides within.

Only *you* can know what is needed in your soul for your own soul fulfillment.

Only *you* can be the giver of your own truth.

It is a feeling, a knowingness; to *know* your truth is also to *feel* your truth.

Seek what feels right within your soul.

Believe in yourself.

Be willing to Become unlimited in your truth, remembering, always, that truth is ongoing, evolving, being created every moment by every thought you have.

While there is a paradox associated with truth, it is also a profound truth, no matter how contradictory it may appear.

When you have come to understand that *everything* is true and yet *nothing* is true, you shall be able to see that just as you perceive truth to be whatever you determine it to be, so may all.

In continuation of this explanation, in the moment that you no longer give credence to a truth, it is no longer real, for you have since moved toward a new truth.

When you come to understand that truth *is* and *can be* all things, then you are free, no longer enslaved to laws, rules, dogma or intellectual understanding.

To learn to Become multi-faceted in your truth means that you are not *one* truth, but *all* truths.

Become who and what you truly are by *listening to the God within you*.

Become who and what you truly are by both knowing and accepting that *God speaks through feelings*, for they will be your guide to truth, directing you onward toward your individual path of enlightenment.

Love and Compassion

Love is your purpose. Compassion is your birthright. Compassion is your truest nature.

The keys to compassion lie in your ability to embrace *all* experiences as part of the one, without judgment.

This is the greatest challenge that all must face as they move towards greater states of personal mastery, which is the return to your truest form.

Compassionate allowing is the gift we give to another.

Demonstrating love through compassionate allowing means that you must love others enough to *allow* the range of their experience.

Compassion allows you to view from an equal standpoint.

Compassion is what you *allow* yourself to Become.

There is no judgment.

All people express their own versions of compassion through the manner in which they conduct themselves in every waking moment.

Are you willing to forgive those who have wronged you?

Are you willing to see beyond hate towards those who oppress you?

It is only in answering yes to these questions that you can choose to Become *more than* the circumstances.

In breaking the cycles of collective response, one becomes the higher choice.

Mastery of compassion means redefining what your world means to you.

It is *not* about forcing change upon the world around you.

You, and only you, choose *how* you respond.

As a being of compassion, you are offered the opportunity to *transcend polarity while still living within the polarity*.

This is what enables you to move forward with life, a life filled with freedom, resolution and peace.

Compassion means living in trust.

Compassion means living with joy.

Living a new truth must first start with the individual. You must have the wisdom and the courage to embrace this new life, this new truth, as your reality.

This reality must then be lived in a world that may not always support that truth. Was not this the undertaking of the entire earthly mission of Yeshua (Jesus)?

Life is a spiritual endeavor. You are asked to become that which you most desire in your life.

Become the peace that you seek.

Become the compassion that you desire.

Become the forgiveness that you seek.

Become the love that you desire.

Be *not afraid* to demonstrate your Becoming. The healing of this world will come about as a result of the healing of thoughts, feelings and emotions.

Who among you is willing to live the truth of a higher response?

Who among you is willing to live the truth of what life has always had to offer?

By virtue of your service to yourself and others, so, too, do you serve the Creator. In this way, you Become the greatest gift that you can offer.

Your ability to express forgiveness, allowing others the outcome of *their* own experiences, without changing the nature of who you truly are, is the highest level of mastery to which you can attain.

Therein lies the healing of all illusion, all separation, all duality.

I will say, once again, *be not afraid* to demonstrate your Becoming.

Complete Trust in the Force

The main rule of conscious creation is this: *you are the creator of your own reality.*

This means, of course, that everything you have experienced in your life has been your own creation; likewise, it also means that anything you wish to create in your own life is never further away than your own thoughts (in combination with both feelings and emotions).

You are the creator of your reality *because you are the chooser of the thought*, right now, at this given moment.

In fact, interaction "is for the purpose of experiencing ourselves: in you, I get to see a part of myself, in me you get to see a part of yourself. Relating with me is a chance for you to discover yourself and relating with you is a chance for me to discover myself. We are all mirrors for one another. Everyone and everything you see in your world is a reflection of what goes on within. This is how we experience life." [414]

However, because we live "in a mass culture where meaning is centralized, we are used to having others interpret our lives for us. We have become passive observers of our own experience, waiting for other people to tell us what it means. Outside influences so often direct our attention to what we should care about and what we should strive for, that the truth of our own power escapes us." [415]

Interestingly enough, there really is "no intrinsic meaning to anything. In most cases we did not consciously choose the meanings we give to things. Rather, they were taught to us, according to the conventions of our culture and our family, when we were too small to know any better. The great news is that we could have consciously chosen our own meanings if we had wanted to, and that, in fact, is just what people

---

[414] *Being a Creator or Reality: Position of Omnipotence* article accessed on November 18, 2011 at http://www.mindreality.com/being-a-creator-of-reality-position-of-omnipotence
[415] *Become the Creator of Your Own Reality* article accessed on November 18, 2011 at http://www.mindpowernews.com/Creator.htm

who are continually happy and peaceful have learned to do." [416]

This means, as has already been stated, that you are the creator of your own reality. In addition, it also means that "this principle has a corollary: you will be able to make wise and resourceful choices to the extent that you live consciously rather than unconsciously. If you have become an automatic response mechanism, unthinkingly adopting those responses chosen or you by your culture and society, then your inner journey will be stalled. If, on the other hand, you are able to wake up and become more aware of what moves and motivates you, you will see that you have picked up the paintbrush; you are painting the shapes of your feelings on that blank canvas. What you are painting is as ephemeral as anything else in life, but the lines you draw, the shapes you form, and the colors you choose, are what give your life meaning." [417]

---

[416] *Become the Creator of Your Own Reality* article accessed on November 18, 2011 at http://www.mindpowernews.com/Creator.htm
[417] Ibid.

As a more conscious being, knowing that you create the world you inhabit, you begin to understand your own power. While you "have some ability to change what is, there are real limits to what you can do." [418]

This is when you are able to acknowledge that "your power comes from how you respond to what is, not from misguided attempts to control what is. How things are for you is, to a great extent, the product of how you feel about what is happening, and how you feel is the result of the meaning you have placed on what is happening." [419]

For me, the greatest wisdom lies in knowing how to listen in the silence, to meditate, and consequently act (out of truth and honesty) on the information that is received.

10 Epic Quotes from *Conversations With God* [420]

---

[418] *Become the Creator of Your Own Reality* article accessed on November 18, 2011 at http://www.mindpowernews.com/Creator.htm
[419] Ibid.
[420] http://www.highexistence.com/10-epic-quotes-from-conversations-with-god/

A Universe Made of Consciousness (Interview with Lynne McTaggart) [421]

Cause or Accident? [422]

Consciousness, Causality and Quantum Physics [423]

Create Your Own Reality [424]

Create Your Own Reality in 6 Steps [425]

Get Your Ki (Qi) Moving with Brain Wave Vibration [426]

Quantum Thoughts [427]

---

[421]

http://www.soundstrue.com/articles/A_Universe_Made_of_Conscious ness-An_Interview_with_Lynne_McTaggart/

[422]

http://www.shamanschool.com/resources/articles/causeoraccident.html

[423] http://www.bibliotecapleyades.net/esp_paradigmaholo06.htm

[424] http://www.lawofattraction123.com/create-your-own-reality.html

[425] http://www.pluginid.com/create-your-own-reality/

[426] http://www.qi-journal.com/Qigong.asp?Name=Get Your Ki (Qi) Moving with Brain Wave vibration&-token.D=Article

[427] http://www.balancedexistence.com/quantum-thoughts/

The Amazing Promises of the Zero Point Field [428]

The Awakening Shift [429]

The Dan Brown Phenomenon [430]

The God Theory [431]

The Intention Experiment [432]

The Law of Personal Creation [433]

The Master Method Blog: You Are the Creator of Your Own Reality [434]

---

[428]

http://www.odemagazine.com/doc/8/the_amazing_promises_of_the_zero_point_field/

[429] http://www.theawakeningshift.com/tag/zero-point-field/

[430] http://www.philipcoppens.com/ls_2.html

[431] http://www.thegodtheory.com/questionsanswers.htm

[432] http://www.theintentionexperiment.com/the-experiments

[433] http://www.creategoodthings.com/inner-temple/the-law-of-personal-creation

[434] http://marco-sies.blogspot.com/2011/08/you-are-creator-of-your-own-reality.html

The Path of Power, Awakening and Enlightenment: The Zero Point [435]

The Primacy of Consciousness [436]

The Zero Point Field and Law of Resonance [437]

You Are The Only Creator Of Your Life Experience [438]

You Create Your Own Reality [439]

Zero Point Energy and the Nature of Consciousness [440]

---

[435] http://www.thepathofpower.org/enlightenment/the-zero-point
[436] http://www.peterrussell.com/SP/PrimConsc.php
[437] http://www.tokenrock.com/secret_resonance/zeropoint_field.php
[438] http://reinis.drupalgardens.com/book/export/html/272
[439] http://www.counsellingforyourself.co.uk/page4.html
[440] http://catchingyourbreath.blogspot.com/2011/07/zero-point-energy-and-nature-of.html

Detachment

It is written in the <u>Ashtavakra Gita</u>, an ancient Sanskrit sacred text, that *one who has finally learned that it is in the nature of objects to come and go without ceasing, rests in detachment and is no longer subject to suffering.* [441]

Detachment, then, refers to one who has overcome his or her attachment to many aspects, such as fear, anger, jealousy, guilt, frustration, control, the ego, falsehood, people, ownership, material things, belief systems, a false sense of security, outcomes, emotions and situations; meaning, in short, that this person has attained a heightened perspective.

Ashtavakra Gita [442]

Attachment and Detachment [443]

---

[441] http://www.wisdomforthesoul.org/categories/detachment.html

[442] http://www.realization.org/page/doc0/doc0004.htm

[443] http://www.srichinmoy.org/resources/library/talks/human_experience/attachment_detachment/index.html

---

[444] http://www.jodyrosehelfand.com/apps/blog/show/6161621
[445]
http://www.laughteryoga.org/index.php?option=com_content&view=article&id=1300:attachments-in-life-stops-us-from-laughing&catid=213:my-diary&Itemid=460
[446]
http://www.berzinarchives.com/web/en/archives/approaching_buddhism/introduction/basic_question_detachment_nonviolence_compassion.html
[447] http://www.athilat.com/bkwsu/Detachment.htm
[448]
http://www.abichal.com/html/spirituality/srichinmoy/ckg_writings/Detachment.htm
[449] http://www.successconsciousness.com/index_000066.htm
[450] http://www.livestrong.com/article/14712-developing-detachment/

Emotional Detachment Can Improve Your Life [451]

Law of Detachment: Flowing with God [452]

Practicing Detachment [453]

The Heart of Awareness [454]

The Law of Detachment [455]

The Law of Dharma or Purpose in Life [456]

The Role of Detachment in Spiritual Practice [457]

The Spiritual Lifestyle of Detachment and Attachments [458]

---

[451] http://www.successconsciousness.com/blog/inner-peace/emotional-detachment-can-improve-your-life/

[452] http://www.mindreality.com/law-of-detachment-flowing-with-god

[453] http://www.alexandertechnique.com/articles/zen/

[454] http://bhagavan-ramana.org/ashtavakragita2.html

[455] http://www.chopra.com/laws/detachment

[456] http://www.chopra.com/dailyinspiration

[457] http://consciouslivingprograms.com/2011/02/11/love-and-detachment-how-do-they-fit-part-i/

[458] http://independentspirituality.com/way-non-attachment/

Self Improvement

Self Improvement is what constitutes my spirit training. While soul/spirit training is required if one is to become a Jedi Knight, self improvement is my choice.

A dear friend of mine took the time to share these words of wisdom ... Last night I awoke from a deep sleep; not startled, but rather peaceful. I felt a smile, which is quite unusual for me. I am considered a 'grump' because I seldom smile. I had gone to bed thinking about all the things I *have to do*, and how there is simply, physically, no possible way that I can complete everything. Then, I came to the realization: I have such a full life. I have done nearly everything I wanted to do and I learn something new every day. This was followed by the revelation: I am able to live such a life because I *have so much to do*. I actually have what I want (a fulfilling life), but was only seeing it as an impossible amount of work.

This is *exactly* the type of mindset that we need to make our way back to.

We are here to learn to become more compassionate and more altruistic, for the betterment of ourselves and our human brethren.

It is also most interesting to denote that Jedi comes from "an ancient Egyptian word *Djedi* (*Djeheuti*) … [which is] a name attributed to an early Egyptian God with those identical humanitarian characteristics and bound by similar heritage and discipline." [459]

May the Force always be with you.

---

[459] Vayro, Ian Ross. (2006) *They Lied To Us in Sunday School* (page 375). Queensland, Australia: Joshua Books.

2012: Another Perspective

In the words of Sri Kalki Bhagavan …

Most of you know that the earth has got a magnetic field. As the earth's molten core is rotating; the magnetic field is created.

The thought sphere of the human mind is located in the earth's magnetic field. This magnetic field has been weakening dramatically over the last ten years.

In physics, there is a parameter called Schumann's Resonance. Using this, we can determine the strength of the earth's magnetic field.

For many centuries, it was constant, around 7.80 cycles per second, but during the last 7-8 years, it has risen to 11 cycles per second and is continuing to increase dramatically. If you work it out mathematically, it appears that, by the year 2012, the Schuman's Resonance is likely to be 13 cycles per second.

When this resonance is 13 cycles per second, the earth's core would stop rotating, and with the magnetic field gone, your mind is gone.

When I say *your mind*, what I mean is your *samskaras*. The pressure of the past 11,000 years of samskaras will vanish.

In Dharma, we also say, *Mind is Karma*. All actions start from your mind. The mind is nothing but a storehouse of samskaras or past life vasanas from which all action emanates.

This is stored in the earth's magnetic field. So in the year 2012, it will become zero for a few days. After that, the core will start rotating again.

This would be a fresh beginning for man or the dawn of the Golden Age. This is the significance of the year 2012.

How do we know, it will happen? The study of fossil records has shown that, it happens roughly after 11,000 years.

It's only a short time away and then we can all start afresh. That is why I want you to become enlightened by 2012.

If you are enlightened, with all your samskaras gone, we can begin a new yuga, which can be called Sathya Yuga or the Golden Age. Man will enter into a new state of altered consciousness.

The earth's resonance is increasing which means the earth's heart is undergoing a transformation. The earth has got a physical body, like you have a body. It has a consciousness as well. As the resonance is increasing, the earth's heart is functioning very differently from before. It is at this time that your heart and the earth's heart are connected.

The earth's heart can be influenced by your heart and vice versa. That is why, it is essential that your heartbeat synchronises with the earth's resonance. This means your heart must flower.

Your heart will flower when you discover love in your relationships.

To discover love, you must stop judging your parents, spouses, etc., internally. Nobody can be judged as the whole universe directly influences all events, even the behaviour of the people.

So learn to experience life. Life has to be experienced, be it pain or pleasure. [460]

460

http://www.ammabhagavan.net/significance_of_2012_by_amma_bhagavan.php

Noetic Jediism

Noetic Jediism consists of two interlocking conceptual keys.

Noetic can be defined as innate knowing, or *intrinsically of the mind.* Jediism has been depicted as an ethical mystic practice concerned with the guardianship of perpetual civilization in the cosmos, a spiritual path that bridges the present dichotomous gulf between science and religion via evidence-based spiritual practice. [461]

As such, our path is informed both by science and individual intuition. These keys depart radically from centripetal control schemes and the dogma and personality cults surrounding individuals so familiar in the world's major religions and cults. [462]

The only dogma here is common sense, making sense, and collectively striving to identify and align with behaviors, broadly expressed as spiritual practices, that align ourselves

---

[461] http://www.noeticjedi.org/we-are-postmodern-scientific-shamans
[462] Ibid.

geometrically with the means and ends of mutual upliftment and environmental caretaking; hence, we become sovereign individuals, each responsible exactly for ourselves, independent of masters or slaves, mindful of our fit with Nature and resonant with Source. [463]

---

[463] http://www.noeticjedi.org/we-are-postmodern-scientific-shamans

Jedi Religion and Matrixism

As per The Jedi Moon article [464] ……

The Jedi religion and Matrixism both speak to the growing discontent with previous religious dogma and also, in my opinion, to a increasing yearning for spiritual answers to the questions that modernity has left unanswered.

Of these two pop culture based religions Jediism seems to be more complete in that it professes (or at least claims) that its moral and spiritual code is of its own design. Matrixism, on the other hand, leaves much of a personal moral code to what has been written in previous religions. Perhaps this is more honest in that most of what the Jedi religion professes has been borrowed from other religions and codes.

---

[464] http://www.geocities.ws/matrixism/moon.html

Matrixism is also connected to previous major and minor religions in that it carries with the legacy of a Messianic prophecy. This prophecy is not only common to Christianity and Judaism, but it is also common to Buddhism, Hinduism, The Baha'i Faith, Islam and a host of new religions and traditional indigenous religions.

Matrixism seems to be stronger, in two particular ways, than Jediism.

The first is that it makes an attachment to previous major religions. This could be important in gaining serious followers from other religions especially those of an Abrahamic lineage.

Secondly, Matrixism carries with it a new and potentially better sacrament. It is quite probable that communion has a very important role in the formation and stability of religious communities. Psilocybin has been shown to foster genuine spiritual experience and it has also been shown to combat depression.

It is my intention here to compare and contrast these two examples of fiction based religions.

The first thing one notices when comparing these two new religious movements is that there is a marked difference in the number of varieties.

While there are numerous websites claiming to represent The Jedi Religion, with no one definitive site taking the lead, there seems to be only one very prominent example of Matrixism. This may be due to the fact that Star Wars movies have been around for a much longer period of time than have The Matrix films.

The next difference that comes to mind is that of theology.

The Jedi religion, in almost all cases, seems to be closely related to Taoism. Matrixism, however, is clearly an Abrahamic tradition with new religious laws and its own prophet (albeit an anonymous one).

This brings up another interesting difference.

The Jedi Religion bases itself mainly on the films, sometimes sighting a loose affiliation with Taoism. Matrixism, by virtue of some quotes concerning "the matrix" from the scripture of the Baha'i Faith, tries to bind itself more tightly to religious history.

There are, of course, major differences in doctrine, also.

Matrixism subscribes to what are called the "Four Tenets" while The Jedi Religion relies on the chivalrous code of medieval Europe.

In total, Matrixism has four tenets and seven laws. The Jedi Religion, in contrast, has a code of anywhere from four to twenty-one sayings or virtues.

One significant thing that both Matrixism and The Jedi religion have in common is that they both openly welcome believers of other religions.

For example, it is perfectly okay to be a Christian and a Matrixist or a Jedi and Hindu at the same time.

More than 70,000 Australians and 390,000 Britons heeded the call to action and recorded Jedi as their religion in the 2001 National Census.

While the majority of people claiming affiliation to Jediism probably did so in a spirit of fun and/or rebellion, research suggests there are members of society who take the 'religion' quite seriously.

A religion is regarded as a set of beliefs and practices, usually involving acknowledgment of a divine or higher being or power, by which people order the conduct of their lives both practically and in a moral sense.

[According to the Temple of the Jedi Order, situated in Texas, USA] Jediism is both an old and new religion; we did the same thing that religions have done for thousands of years ... we assimilated spiritual teachings from other and ancient faiths: Taoism, Zen Buddhism, Mysticism, as well as the honourable martial arts philosophies; this spiritual mixture is potent.

We call this fusion Jediism.

The Jedi Code transcends racial, class and gender boundaries by promoting universal values or sentiments and, in the present climate of fear and uncertainty, may offer a panacea to the troubles that some see as being associated with mainstream organised religion.

Jedi are the guardians of peace and justice throughout the World.

Jedi use their powers to defend and protect, never to attack others.

Jedi respect all life, in all its forms, they are humble and live to serve all living things.

For the good of others, Jedi seek to improve themselves through knowledge and wisdom, a journey that never ends.

The Jedi teachings are the yellow brick road to modern day Christian living. Where the Bible uses parables, the Jedi teachings use a direct approach. However, both also correlate with each other, going hand in hand, neither contradicting the other.

Being a Christian means, I love the Lord and follow his Word; being a Jedi means, I constantly seek knowledge and enlightenment.

In an interview with <u>Time Magazine</u> in 1999, George Lucas, the director of the Star Wars series of films, stated that it was not his intention to instigate a new religious movement as a result of the inclusion of religious themes in Star Wars but rather to: try to awaken a certain kind of spirituality in young people, more a belief in God than a belief in any particular religious system.

While it may not have been Lucas's plan to instigate a new religion, the Jedi phenomena is evidence that, intentional or unintentional, religious references in popular culture can have the effect of solidifying beliefs.

Lucas describes what he believes to be the attraction of the Jedi: *I'm telling an old myth in a new way. Each society takes that myth and retells it in a different way, which relates to the particular environment they live in. The motif is the same. It's just that it gets localized. As it turns out, I'm localizing it for the planet. I guess I'm localizing it for the end of the millennium more than I am for any particular place.*

REFERENCES

http://templeofthejediorder.org/

http://www.thejediencyclopedia.com/theforce.php?Section= Background

Of Myth and Men: A conversation between Bill Moyers and George Lucas on the meaning of the Force and the true theology of Star Wars, Time Magazine, 153: 16, 26 April 1999 Murray, B. (2004).

http://www.ons.gov.uk/ons/rel/census/census-2001-summary-theme-figures-and-rankings/390-000-jedis-there-are/index.html

http://www.abs.gov.au/Websitedbs/D3110124.NSF/24e5997 b9bf2ef35ca2567fb00299c59/86429d11c45d4e73ca256a400 006af80!OpenDocument

http://en.wikipedia.org/wiki/Jedi_census_phenomenon

Jediism Links

21 Maxims of the Jediism Code [465]

33 Jedi Teachings to Live By [466]

A Way to the Force [467]

Basic Teachings of the Jedi [468]

Finding Your Master Teacher [469]

Force Teachings [470]

Guardians of the Jedi Order [471]

---

[465] http://setiishadim.wordpress.com/2007/01/12/21-maxims-of-the-jediism-code/
[466] http://altreligion.about.com/od/jedireligion/tp/33-Jedi-Teachings-To-Live-By.htm
[467]

http://www.quantumlight.com/theforce/writings/force/the_force.htm
[468]

http://altreligion.about.com/od/beliefsandcreeds/a/jedi_teachings.htm
[469] http://cosmicascension.com/Finding_Your_Master_Teacher.html
[470] http://www.raptorsquad.net/force/forceteach/index.html
[471] http://gjoguardians.wikidot.com/code-tenets

How to Live the Jedi Way [472]

How to Train the Jedi Way [473]

International Church of Jediism Members Forum [474]

Jedi Academy Online [475]

Jedi Census Phenomenon [476]

Jedi Church (New Zealand) [477]

Jedi Foundation [478]

Jedi Lifestyle [479]

Jedi Manual Basic: Introduction to Jedi Knighthood [480]

---

[472] http://kincharbamin.com/Live-Like-A-Jedi.html
[473] http://io9.com/5048816/become-a-jedi-knight-in-one-easy-lesson
[474] http://churchofjediism.grou.ps/home
[475] http://www.jediacademyonline.com/jcircle2.html
[476] http://en.wikipedia.org/wiki/Jedi_census_phenomenon
[477] http://www.jedichurch.org/
[478] http://jedifoundation.com/jedicircle.html
[479] http://cosmicascension.com/Jedi_Lifestyle.html
[480] http://www.amazon.com/dp/B002G1ZT2A/

Jedi Manual Intermediate: The Path of Truth [481]

Jedi Manual Mastery: Path of the Immortals [482]

Jedi Philosophy [483]

Jedi Religion [484]

Jedi Resource Center [485]

Jedi Training [486]

Jedi Website [487]

Jediism [488]

---

[481] http://www.amazon.com/dp/B00507CU92/
[482] http://www.amazon.com/dp/B005IQKV00/
[483] http://kitoba.com/pedia/Jedi%20Philosophy.html
[484]
http://altreligion.about.com/od/alternativereligionsaz/a/jedi_religion.ht
m
[485] http://jediresourcecenter.org/vb/
[486] http://cosmicascension.com/Jedi_Training.html
[487] http://jediorganization.addr.com/jedi/website/
[488] http://www.jediism.org/

Jediism: A 21st Century Paradigm [489]

Jediism Forum [490]

Jedi Philosophy [491]

Jedi Religion (Jediism) [492]

Jedi Temple Philosophy [493]

May the Force Be with You [494]

My Case Against Jediism [495]

New Jediism Order [496]

---

[489] http://mbarwelluk.posterous.com/jediism-a-new-way-of-looking-at-older-faiths
[490] http://www.forumjar.com/forums/Jediism
[491] http://kitoba.com/pedia/Jedi%20Philosophy.html
[492]
http://altreligion.about.com/od/alternativereligionsaz/a/jedi_religion.htm
[493]
http://templeofthejediforce.org/modules/newbb/viewforum.php?forum=2
[494] http://ijedi.co.uk/
[495] http://community.beliefnet.com/go/thread/view/43861/22838221/
[496] http://www.newjediismorder.org/index.html

Noetic Order of Jedi [497]

Order of the Jedi (a Canadian website) [498]

Real Jedi Knights [499]

Temple of the Jedi Order [500]

The Church of Jediism (UK) [501]

The Earth Jedi Order [502]

The Force Holocron: 21 Maxims of the Jediism Code [503]

The Force in Jediism [504]

The Institute for Jedi Realist Studies [505]

---

[497] http://www.noeticjedi.org/
[498] http://www.orderofthejedi.org/
[499] http://jediknights.b1.jcink.com/index.php?act=idx
[500] http://templeofthejediforce.org/modules/newbb/index.php
[501] http://www.churchofjediism.org.uk/Home.html
[502] http://www.communigate.co.uk/ne/earthjedi2/index.phtml
[503] http://setiishadim.wordpress.com/2007/01/12/21-maxims-of-the-jediism-code/
[504] http://altreligion.about.com/od/beliefsandcreeds/p/force.htm
[505] http://instituteforjedirealiststudies.org/library/52-jc.html

The Jedi Book [506]

The Jedi Code [507]

The Jedi Creed [508]

The Jedi Doctrine [509]

The Jedi Encyclopedia [510]

The Jedi Manual [511]

The Jedi Path [512]

The Jedi Path: A Manual for Students of the Force [513]

---

[506] http://thejedibook.webs.com/thejedibook.htm
[507] http://www.angelfire.com/rpg/jks/jedicode.html
[508] http://www.jedicreed.org/
[509] http://jedism.wall.fm/forum/topic/1
[510]

http://www.thejediencyclopedia.com/theforce.php?Section=Background

[511] http://thejedimanual.webs.com/jedi101.htm
[512] http://www.amazon.com/dp/1452102279/
[513] http://www.amazon.com/dp/1603800964/

The Jedi Sanctuary Training Guide [514]

The Jedi Temple [515]

The Jedi United Organization [516]

The Jedi Way: A Course in Training [517]

The Jediism Way [518]

The Maryland Jedi Order [519]

The Modern Jedi Knight [520]

The Tao of Yoda [521]

The Way of Jediism [522]

---

[514] http://www.amnesy.it/Downloads/Grafica/Jedi%20Sanctuary-Training%20Guide.pdf
[515] http://www.jedi-temple.org/2010/01/harmony-force/
[516] http://www.freewebs.com/jediunited/jedicircle.htm
[517] http://setiishadim.wordpress.com/2007/02/09/the-jedi-way-a-course-of-training/
[518] http://jediism.tripod.com/
[519] http://www.marylandjedi.org/
[520] http://www.modernjediknight.com/MJK_history.html
[521] http://sci-fi.lovetoknow.com/wiki/The_Tao_of_Yoda
[522] http://library.templeofthejediorder.org/TheWayofJediism.pdf

The Ways of the Jedi [523]

Vad Ar Jediism [524]

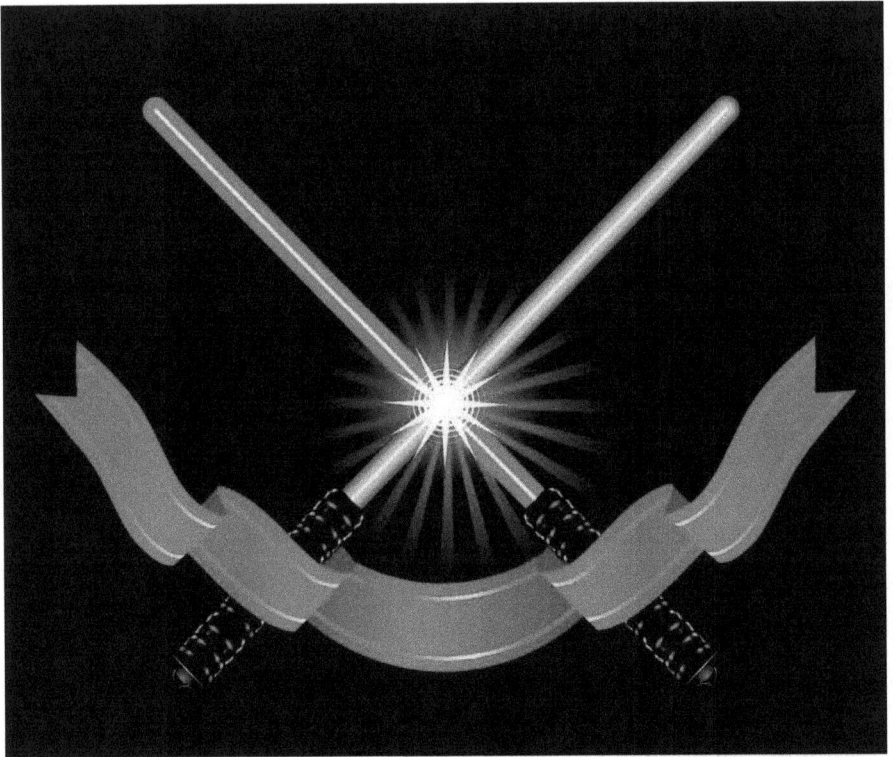

---

[523] http://switz.tripod.com/jedi.html
[524] http://www.totjfsweden.n.nu/vad-ar-jediism

About the Author

Michele Doucette is webmistress of Portals of Spirit, a spirituality website whereby one will find links to [1] The Enlightened Scribe, [2] an ezine called Gateway To The Soul, [3] books of spiritual resonance as well as authors of metaphysical importance, [4] categories of interest from Angels to Zen, [5] up-to-date information as shared by a Quantum Healer, [6] affiliate programs and resources of personal significance, [7] healing resource advertisements and [8] spiritual news.

As a Level 2 Reiki Practitioner, she sends long distance Reiki to those who make the request, claiming only to be a facilitator of the Universal energy, meaning that it is up to the individual(s) in question to use these energies in order to heal themselves.

Having also acquired a Crystal Healing Practitioner diploma (Stonebridge College in the UK), she is guardian to many from the mineral kingdom.

She is the author of several spiritual/metaphysical works; namely, [1] *The Ultimate Enlightenment For 2012: All We Need Is Ourselves*, a book that was nominated for the Allbooks Review Best Inspirational Book for 2011, [2] *Turn Off The TV: Turn On Your Mind*, [3] *Veracity At Its Best*, [4] *The Collective: Essays on Reality* (a composition of essays in relation to the Matrix), [5] *Sleepers Awaken: The Time Is Now To Consciously Create Your Own Reality*, [6] *Healing the Planet and Ourselves: How To Raise Your Vibration*, [7] *You Are Everything: Everything Is You*, [8] *The Awakening of Humanity: A Foremost Necessity*, [9] *The Cosmos of the Soul: A Spiritual Biography* and [10] *Getting Out Of Our Own Way: Love Is The Only Answer*, all of which have been published through St. Clair Publications.

In addition, she has written a separate volume that deals with crystals, aptly entitled *The Wisdom of Crystals*.

She is also the author of *A Travel in Time to Grand Pré*, a visionary metaphysical novel that historically ties the descendants of Yeshua (Jesus) to modern day Nova Scotia.

As shared by a reviewer, it is *Veracity At Its Best*, a spiritual (metaphysical) tome, that "constructs the context for the spiritual message" imparted in *A Travel in Time to Grand Pré*.

Against the backdrop of 1754 Acadie, it was the blending of French Acadian history with current DNA testing that contributed to the weaving of this alchemical tale of time travel, romance and intrigue.

From Henry I Sinclair to the Merovingians, from the Cathari treasure at Montségur to the Knights Templar, this novel, together with the words of Yeshua as spoken at the height of his ministry, has the potential to inspire others; for it is herein that we learn how individuals can find their way, their truth(s), so as to live their lives to the fullest.

Likewise, she has also recently published *Back Home with Evangeline*, the long awaited sequel to *A Travel in Time to Grand Pré*.

www.ingramcontent.com/pod-product-compliance
Lightning Source LLC
Chambersburg PA
CBHW051951090426
42741CB00008B/1349